Essence

Essence

An Exploration of the Conscious Universe

***

Thomas F. Radzienda

SOVEREIGN WORD
PUBLISHING

Essence

Published by

Sovereign Word Publishing
Chiang Mai, Thailand

Cataloguing in Publication Data

National Library of Thailand

Radzienda, Thomas F.
Essence / Chiang Mai / Createspace / 2017
188 pp.

1. Meditation. 2. Yoga. I. Title.
158.12

ISBN

978-616-429-587-2

For Frank and Nancy Radzienda
whose Essence forever remains with me

Eternal Grace

The eternal Grace within me wishes to reach out and nourish the eternal Grace within you.

The Spirit of the Universe

The spirit of the Universe is already perfect.

Unconditional Love

Unconditional love for yourself will release you from the desire for perfection. Loving yourself is the primary expression of Universal love.

The Plague

Criticism can be a horrible plague. This is exactly what
spreads when we judge others. We project self-criticism onto
other people in order to enhance our own self-image.

Irrelevant Expectations

Self-acceptance makes approval superfluous. It makes the
expectations of others entirely irrelevant.

Independence

Focusing on the ego-self limits the ability to know and
accept the totality of what we are. Acceptance of self needs
to be complete and unconditional. Unconditional love of self
is non-judgmental. Self-acceptance is independent of
cultural, religious or social demands. The goal is acceptance
of self as we truly exist. And now, liberate yourself even
from the notion of independence.

Unconditional Acceptance

The burns on my legs and the scars on my heart remain with me until I unconditionally accept myself as I am. Acceptance of self is a precursor to acceptance of the world. First, I must stop judging myself and this world. I simply need to accept it. By accepting the world, I am in tune with it rather than condemning it.

Self-Defence

The ego defends the small individual self, thereby handicapping awareness of the Universal Essence of self. If we do not accept self as it is, of course we need the ego to defend us. The ego that we create to protect our weak self can be very aggressive.

Fear of the World

The ego does not accept the world because the world is perceived as a threat. The ego-self establishes unrealistic expectations of the world. The ego criticizes and refuses to accept the world as it is in order to guarantee the grandiosity of the ego.

Fasting the Ego

Fasting weakens my ego-drive to change the world, leaving me with only enough energy and stamina to purify. Fasting this body contributes to minimizing the ego. Fasting nourishes the spirit. It opens spiritual channels of awareness. Fasting makes it easier for awareness of total Universal self to be experienced.

Spiritual Innovation

From the Universal perspective of the total self, the customs of the ego-self (cultural and national norms) seem frivolous. The futile efforts of the ego-self are laughable. Illusions of inferiority and superiority are in vain. Through spiritual innovation, we can transcend the triviality of the ego.

Awareness of Total Self

'Leave go of the ego' is better described as 'be aware of the total self.' By making this shift in perspective, the ego can be seen more accurately for what it is: a minor part of Universal soul. The ego-self is necessary, fair enough, to protect the enfeebled inner child who has grown up with an isolated perspective within the paradigm of the narrow world of individualism.

From Inner Self to God-Self

What is the nature of self? Is it a continuum embracing everything from myself to yourself, from non-self to God-self?

Transcendence

Can we conceive of God as the structural level beyond the Universe? In this paradigm, God is not considered an entity. God is that which transcends the Universe and all conceptualizations.

Humanity is an Incarnation of Self

Is there reincarnation of self? Are there multiple, simultaneous incarnations of self?

All simultaneous and linear incarnations are aspects of the total, Universal self. Once unconditional acceptance and love of self has been established, Universal love of humanity emerges because all of humanity is an incarnation of self.

The World is my Larger Self

All the evil that I see in the world is actually a part of me, just as I am part of the world. That's why it frustrates me to struggle to change the world. I am the world in all its glory and all its folly. The world is my larger self.

Steady Awareness

With steady awareness of all the dimensions within the Universal self, it becomes easier to improve things. Why? Because the only thing that we are truly capable of changing is self. Within the Universal Being are the small, local selves of billions. Each is a minor part of Universal self. Step by step we can evolve.

Here

Acceptance at Dawn

I begin each dawn by accepting myself exactly as I am. I'm learning to love myself without condition. I demonstrate love to myself in every way I can. From this acceptance and love I begin to accept others exactly as they truly are.

The Unloved is the Evil

The remaining evils in the world are the unloved and unaccepted aspects of the Universal self.

Approval is Optional

Approval is optional. All along, I had expected the world to approve of me. I finally realized that I simply needed to accept the world. This was my 180-degree turn around. Smile!

Divine Right

What remains of our divine right to be?

Stately Illusions

What has happened to our ability to perceive beyond the shadows cast by stately illusions?

Sovereign

Unfettered by titles and degrees, unencumbered by papers and documented trails, we are Sovereign.

In Search of Itself

Does mind recognize that awareness is the Universe in search of itself?

The Most Important Asana

The most important asana in all of Yoga is the smile. Your
smile is a season in itself.

One Leaf

In one leaf fallen from a tree, read the secrets of the forest.
In one stone on the path, hold the Essence of the mountain.

Intuition

Nature is poetry, expressed through perfect intuition. Poetry
is nature, expressed through perfect awareness.

The Poetic Leap

The very nature of poetry is to leap beyond the grasp of
what it is supposed to be.

The Signature

The soul is the Essence of delicate, invisible fruit. The
signature of my soul is a poem.

Faithful Silence

To hear the eternal song of the Universe requires infinite
silence of the mind.

The Whisper

Silence resembles the whisper of searching hearts stepping
peacefully from thought to thought.

One Step

Eternity presents itself one step at a time.

The Dance of Now

The dance of now between the Universe and I meets where silence is our most precious melody.

Silence is Wiser than Thought

Carry me to the river where the children of the stream are quieter than the whisper of the leaves. Teach me - silently - to be the stream.

When to the River

Can I walk unfettered through the autumn leaves?
Breathing the chilly mountain breeze and
Be, just - simply walking being -
Not on a path or crusade
Not coveting insight, simply —

Walking Be

Unattached to the illusions of my own grandeur
Unsure of the boundary and depth of my being
Never certain whether I am on the path or the incarnate path
Being peace as silently as dusk
With neither reasons nor goals, purely -

Smiling Be

Not materializing the mystical realm
Just accepting, being here
Neither proving nor denying
Decreeing nor decrying
Righting nor wronging, merely —

Gentle Be

In silence - knowing by smiling
Teaching by listening, learning by sharing
Equilibrium without measure
Every sense firmly contoured within and around me
In the absence of self, solely -

Silent Be

The autumn breeze whispering
Secrets of death to morning flowers
Caressing golden leaves still on the branch
Fluffing the thinning hairs still on my head
Lifting birds too feeble to seek a warmer sun, wisely -

Honey Bee

Eternally in the now of life
Where no compass could point to the truth.

Secrets of the Mountains

Only rivers know the secrets of the mountains;
When to the river, autumn leaves
And every lane is painted like a walk-in Renoir

Who is Feeling?

At breakfast I pondered whether or not I had any control
over my feelings. Can I command myself to 'Have this or
that feeling'? Am I selecting the feelings, or do they have a
life of their own? Do I respond to a stimulus, or does a
response simply occur of its own accord? Is that me?

The Origin of Thoughts

Can I say, ok, now, think about… music. Gershwin and Rachmaninoff spontaneously pop into my mind without any intention. I did not beckon those two names. Thoughts come unsolicited. I did not request those thoughts to occur. Then, who did? From where are the thoughts arising?

These Thoughts are Thinking Me

There is no 'me' to be thinking. I am not thinking any of this. These thoughts are thinking me! These thoughts exist, triggering the attention of me-myself-I to cling and claim authorship.

The Thought of Silence

What accounts for these thoughts being inserted into the silence of my mind?

I will now concentrate on silence. Mystical images occur of their own accord. I see open spaces. The images arise and the commentary continues to run by itself, even as 'I' the thinker claim to be concentrating on silence. This suggests that 'I' have no control over 'my own mind.'

At the Mercy of Thoughts

Am I at the mercy of the thoughts that arrive in my head? Is my life merely a reaction to the thoughts that are presented to me? Can I turn off that function of thoughts arriving on their own, uninvited, by using some kind of mind-spam filter?

I Choose Silence

Silence is my chosen mode. Exquisite silence. Very quickly, thoughts appear in my mind in the same way that itches arise on my skin. Why can't I control these thoughts any more than I can control where an itch will occur?

Vanity

Without opinions, do I still exist? Could we survive in silence and non-opinion? I have read that all opinions are vanity.

Mirrors of Existence

By removing myself from all situations such as the corporation, the university and the nation in an effort to know who I purely am may be impossible because who I am is the very product of those factors. Thus removed, there is nobody remaining. Yet, the ego begins to eke out its existence by forging some new identity all over again.

Who we are Not

Can we only know 'self' vis-à-vis other people and the situations that we experience? Do we know who we are by recognizing who we are not?

We exist, that we are part of a family, culture and history. Removal to a substantial distance opens new boulevards for existence. The greater the geographical and cultural distance, the deeper the potential for new blossoming to occur.

Here

In Absentia

In the beginning, we are the product of family and society.
We perpetuate that being and promote those relations. This
establishes a hall of mirrors. We install mirrors and
kaleidoscopes, and soon confusion clouds our perspective.
In absentia, we look back on those halls and mirrors and see
that all are illusions. The illusions are self-perpetuating and
self-confirming, but lack any relationship to objective reality.

The Mirrorless Universe

Can we exist in the limbo, the vacuum, the mirrorless
Universe? Is the social hall of mirrors the only way by which
to know who we are?

The hall of mirrors is the sum of the illusions projected onto
us plus the images that we project onto others.

Charming Illusions

We create our own reality though the sum of our choices
and non-choices. We create our own selves relative to that
manufactured reality, polishing the mirrors, charming the
illusions, buffing the reflections with all the illusory
enthusiasm of life on the silver screen.

Nature as it Breathes

One way to encourage mindful awareness is to employ
'nature is watching' meditation. This means maintaining
awareness of the moment-to-moment characteristics of
nature as it breathes. Recognize that nature is breathing you.
Continual awareness that nature is breathing is a very
peaceful, mindful observation. It nurtures insight because it
is not self-referent.

Humble Narrator

What is the difference between mindfulness and ego?

Mindfulness is internally silent, not judging, not blaming, and just watching. Mindfulness is the witness. Mindfulness is an innocent, neutral observer. Mindfulness is a humble narrator taking ephemeral notes on the experience of being. Conversely, the ego acts like the hero of every story.

Universe-Referent

What is the difference between mindfulness and self-consciousness?

Self-consciousness is self-referent, whereas mindfulness is Universe-referent.

To Sit or to Share?

I wonder if just sitting and observing is really the ultimate
meditation technique by which to know ourselves and to
experience the truth. Actually, once we have clear vision, it is
helpful to translate ideas into clear thought and expression to
share with others. That said, maybe just walking around,
enlightened, is of benefit to all beings.

Limp Balloons

How many years have been spent running away, working,
drinking, fixing and cleaning, calling and clinging, hoping
and waiting and peering out into the city for friends, into the
country for adventure, into the world for fortune and fame
in the hope of some recognition and acclaim that you are;
you exist; you have value? All of these are ego balloons;
manifestations proving the temporal nature of all
phenomena, all of which deflate with time, like limp balloons
on frazzled strings. That is all that survives of that ego-self
that never truly had the courage to look in the mirror to see
that it did not exist.

Authority

If all of the thoughts that arise in your mind are not under your authority, then how could thought be considered your Essence?

Sacred Mirror of Silence

Run, clean the fridge! Quick, weed the garden! Go, exercise and play! Work, earn, and travel! But never look too deeply into the sacred mirror of silence with mindfulness that penetrates the banality of me-myself-I. The ego-self keeps running, keeps itself inflated, turns the treadmill that primes its pump, bloats its bellows, and in the end, exhausts. In the stench of the funeral pyre lingers the darkest mirror into which it is incumbent for us to witness the void with clarity, recognizing that the illusory self has stolen the show!

Nature Feels

We usually do not have a choice whether to feel, or not to feel; to think or not to think. These phenomena are powers onto themselves. Nature feels, and we interpret those feelings as personal emotion. Consciousness thinks, and we construe that as personal intelligence.

Caretakers of the Universe

Humans are the rhythm of the Universal heart; murmurs of the Universal mind. We sense feelings and experience thoughts on behalf of the Universe. We are caregivers and caretakers of this world and all of its beings. To apprehend this requires profound resolve. The time has arrived for us to perform our roles with sagacity.

An Organ of Serenity

It takes tenacity to hold the mind still, to resist the perpetual temptation to think and analyze more and more. It requires fortitude to hold tight the reins of the heart, embrace them until they are pacified, so this heart may rest in silence: an organ of infinite serenity.

Manifestation

The tranquil mind and serene heart are the ultimate organs
of perception to pierce through the illusions; they function
best in stillness and silence. The moment a personal thought
engages or a feeling persuades, the mind and heart revert
into manifestations of ego forces.

The Agenda Hidden Within

Sit in absolutely perfect inner silence. Can you do it? For five
seconds? Ten seconds? Yes, then, and then, the Universal
mill begins chafing its thoughts and the dust clouds your
vision. A thought arises, unbeckoned. From where did it
come? Did you will it to arise? Can you force it to cease?
OK. One, two, three more seconds of silent stillness and
then what? Another thought arises concerning a chore or a
deed, a question or two about money or food. Again, coming
from where? Maybe it comes from the deep unconscious.
Maybe. Did you call it up? Did you press the 'recall' button
to drum up that memory? Or, is the computer running on its
own momentum; pushing its own buttons; loading its own
programmes… all with an agenda… beyond your conscious
control?

Frontiers of the Soul

Sit in unmitigated for a few more moments. How long before a feeling visits you? A feeling of boredom or anger arises; from where? Did you purposely decide to feel that way? Has it surfaced from within the subconscious? What in the world is that? No one has ever seen or heard, smelled or tasted, measured or photographed such a thing; yet, nearly everybody accepts the notion of the subconscious without question.

How immense would the subconscious be? Where would you discover its frontiers and where would you draw the borders? Who is to say if it is 'yours' or whether it is shared by the millions? Sit in further silence. Allow no feelings to arise and within a moment, a feeling appears. What programme instigates this 'run feelings' function? Is it some backstabbing virus hell-bent on sabotaging your inner peace? How do the feelings persuade you to believe that you are the owner of those feelings?

Who is Driving?

Look into the mirror of this process that you call your life, to times of utter despair. Who chose those feelings back then? Reflect on times of rampant anxiety and random analysis without direction… and who was driving the car of perpetual thought? Can feelings and thoughts really be said to be yours, if it is not you who governs them?

No Exit

Why do I want to answer all of these questions? Why don't I just sit back and nibble on these bananas and listen to the falling rain, and forget all of this existential mumbo jumbo? Because I cannot! I could sooner choose to stop breathing or control the circulation of my blood than get off this mental highway at the next exit. These questions drive me. The questions are searching for a philosopher to sort them out. Is this the Universe striving to know itself?

Candled Darkness

I sit tonight in candled darkness, sandalwood solemnity,
lotus-legged until pain begs for reprieve. Sitting in silence,
watching for clues of meaning. Meaning? What would make
me believe there is any significance to this life? If there is
meaning, what are the chances that an Earth-bound, rational-
empiricist time-slave, three-dimensional human being could
possibly comprehend it?

Sweeping with Equanimity

So why are you so angry? Because anger is here! Just like
happiness is over there. Just like breathing is here and there!
Let it be. Why are we supposed to allow happiness but not
sadness? Why sweep this side of the street, but not the other
side?

The Seer is but a Delusion

With concentrated effort, only the soft rhythm of breathing remains. Then there is the silence. Soon originates the delusion of the self. Then arises the piercing of the deception. Then erupts the freaking out. Soon appears the mirror that does not reflect, for the seer is but a delusion; the self is a convenient construct by which to do the banking and shopping. But the perceiver has no eyes of his own; those are the eyes of the Universe, peering out through his skull. There is no seer, no be-ing, no me. There is only a body, a voice, a façade of behaviour. This is no more authentic than a character in a feature film or any role on Broadway. Seemingly real, rooted in massive verisimilitude, but…

Off Stage

The character is not real, despite being based on a million genuine characteristics of humanity. The role remains a figment of imagination. When off the stage we step, beyond the floodlights into the dark back stage, there, when me-myself-I ceases to be, and all accomplishments and successes of the last 20 or 30 or 40 years are being torn down, scrapped for the next play, melted down for their raw elements, and the me that used to hold that assembly together becomes one with the light and the dark, what then can be said about returning to the stage and perpetuating the drama?

Bound to our Illusions

The audience has long since returned home. The stage hands
are drunkenly delving into their own endeavours. The actors
have reverted to the larger drama that runs 24 hours a day. If
they stepped out of that stage of personification, they would
implode. Call it death of the presumed me-myself-I. Then,
and only then, can rebirth be a possibility. Life beyond death
will only be known when we pass through the barriers that
bind us to our illusions.

The Self is a Provisional Aggregate

The ego assembles various bits and pieces from the
environment; minerals and chemicals, flesh and blood, air
and sea, feelings and thoughts; hopes and memories; family
and culture, time and space, all constructed into an
'aggregate-self' that in its evolution proceeds to consider
itself a solid being. But it is not.

The aggregate-self of me-myself-I is functional, enjoyable,
and purposeful. It is also self-destructive, deluded and
monomaniacal. At best, it is provisional. It gets through the
day, serving its own contrived agenda, based on the faulty
premise that it is an authentic being with real needs and
truth.

Every Cell of the Universe

Any given cell of the physical human structure is a cell of the Universe. Its components have always existed, and always will. The cell will be with the physical body for a month or a year, and then move on. The body-mind aggregate will never know the difference. Even those cells destined to remain for a lifetime will eventually dissolve into their component molecules. And the molecules will perform their various tasks, for a while, and then disperse. But the ego hangs on obstinately.

The Fortress of Psychic Defence

The ego claims ownership and authorship, accepting a provisional name and place to reside; status and goals; builds fortresses in its own psychic defence; resists every attempt to abandon or disown it. It is programmed for one thing: its own survival.

In the silence, see that the aggregate-self is a permeable membrane allowing memories and perceptions to float in and out at will. This aggregate-self perceives danger as it experiences the melding into the Universe. The aggregate-self is part of the Universe, just as a river or mountain. But neither a mountain nor a river draws exclusive borders and claims, 'this is me and that is not.' Only the human aggregate defines itself in such a narrow, reductionist manner.

Briefly Forever

I see. Ok, then, I guess 'I' will just be moving on. This
requires the abandonment of a lifetime of work. Yes, the
lifetime of the aggregate-self, brief in terms of the Universe,
but forever in terms of itself. And what comes after it, if we
fold our personal cards and submit ourselves to Universal
fate? Certainly nothing that the human ego could fathom.
Any notion of significance at the human level is a pittance
relative to the Universal equation. The charade repeats itself
for eons before it evolves itself out of the quagmire. This is
how the Universal life force explores itself.

The Propellers of our Lives

Is it viable that the only way to know my true humanness is
through engagement with society? Is it conceivable that the
best way to experience my true spirit is separated from
society? Is it possible that the social/spiritual dichotomy is
false and misleading? Are separation and engagement but
twin propellers on the shaft that spins our lives?

Grounded

Deep in meditation I was prompted to desist from sitting meditation, to stand up and begin Tai Chi exercises to gain greater understanding of my energy, my balance and my contact with the earth. I followed this intuition and felt renewed, well-grounded, and firmly anchored in this body.

Subtle Whispers

To hear, one must listen. This is obviously true in our social interactions. One who is constantly chatting can hardly be listening very well. Similarly, when the mind is perpetually gossiping with itself, it is impossible to hear the subtle whispers of the Universal soul. Thus, it is imperative to experience silent meditation and listen for the delicate insights that guide us towards our destinations.

Indecision

If certainty were a prerequisite for action, nothing on this planet would ever commence. I've been waiting more than a year to decide whether or not to pursue the path of becoming an energy healer. I waited for certainty until I realized that if decisions required certainty, ambiguity would outlast us all. I have since moved forward into my healing vocation. I can only know the quality of a decision after making it. I cannot judge the merit of a decision by not making any choices. It takes courage to make the decision, especially when we possess imperfect information.

The Universe Explores Itself

Do we exist independently or do we exist only in relation to others?

We actualize when we engage in relationship. Through interactions, we paint the picture of who we are; creating, expressing and sharing, while reflecting on feedback. This creates an inter-being that emerges when the bond commences. Living in isolation does not provide much feedback on the Essence of inter-being. Our social interactions are a genuine dimension of our spiritual evolution. This is how the Universe explores itself.

The Source from which we Spring

What is the value of searching and striving, peering into the darkness and reflecting on our inner Essence? This is the source from which we spring. This is where our roots pierce into the soil of non-existence. Yet, if we dwell too long within the dark soil of the roots, we may get lost in the maze, adrift in thought, and entirely lose sight of our Universal nature. These facets of our being develop in cycles. There is a natural time for delving deep within and a complementary time for reaching out. Honouring these cycles, mindful of their vicissitudes, helps us maintain our balance.

I still Know Nothing

After so much writing, I still do not know what I wish to say. In light of voluminous reading, I still cannot discern what is true. After decades of traveling, I still do not know where I yearn to go. Following thousands of meditations, still so little is clear. Considering an extensive education, I have greater doubts. Is this the paradox? The more I learn, the less I know. The more I travel, the less I see. The more people I meet, the fewer friends I have. The more I meditate, the deeper my ignorance is revealed.

Identity

Am I coming closer to truth as I increasingly encounter
barriers to comprehension? As I meditate more deeply and
intently, I discover how far away I am from inner silence.
Why is it that I cannot say that I am a Buddhist, Christian,
Hindu, Muslim or Jew, an atheist or an agnostic, or simply a
man with his own faith or a man without? I cannot explain
my religion; my nationality; my identity. I do not know who
or what I am.

The Empty House

The inner silence can be so boring; at times relaxing, but
mostly painful and empty. And that's where the truth is? Do
I believe that? If I believe it, why can't I grasp life more
clearly? If not, then what do I believe? Do I no longer even
know what I believe? Once you've cleaned the entire house,
sorted through all the rubbish and given away all the
remainders, you have an empty house. You patch and sand
the walls, paint them peach or blue and settle into an easy
chair that you do not own, to ignore the books that you no
longer believe and discard the opinions that you don't even
hold. I'm not sure there is any big picture, life goal, true self
or anything else in this life. I am not sure of anything. I don't
believe any of my opinions or anybody else's opinions on
anything. I guess.

Can Anybody know Anything?

I have once again swung to an extreme nihilist perspective
and then I gradually nudge myself to some measure of
equilibrium, a balance by which to sort through the present
existence. Then, I delve further into the recognition that
there is no knowing; there is no object to be known; there is
no knower.

I am a Question

If I had any answers, I could get busy as a purveyor of
wisdom. But, instead of that, I cast doubts on every thought
ever held or scribed. Go ahead and say it: the meaning is in
the doubts. The next voice will put it another way: the
doubts are distraction and defilement. Next, we'll hear advice
to trust my intuition. I'm not sure what that implies. I am
more confused than a child landing in a foreign world,
starving and poor, curious and baffled, lonely for friends and
answers, or for a friend with an answer, or at least a friend
with a question by which to entertain us, or a friend that
understands that these questions are all that I have; all that I
am. I am a question.

Arising with the Sun

With neither goals nor regrets, I arise to welcome the sun
with a smile and the veracity to experience the day filled with
neither importance nor boredom. The day just is. Let there
be silence, replete, the only environment within which these
words have any context.

Brevity

The soul never seems to say a word, but it experiences
Essence: indescribable, irrefutable, unswerving, ever
knowing, yet never speaking as many words as written in this
line.

Simply Smile

I already am whatever it is I am, so it is not a decision or an
action to be somebody. Can I simply write to write, be to be?
Can I write in order to perceive what I am? I have a right to
see what I am. Then I can really be. If that involves doing or
not doing is rather insignificant. When asked what I do, I
simply smile.

Intention Empowers

Techniques, methods, systems, mantras and symbols in spiritual practice must be seen for what they are: Tools. These tools are not spiritual in themselves. They are instruments that take time to learn, require discipline to master and insight to understand. In time, we see through the techniques or symbols, realizing that the real power, the real Essence behind them, is our intention: Intention empowers every symbol, mantra or posture that we employ. Without profound spiritual intention, the tools are merely mechanical. Be wary of attachment to symbols, scriptures and procedures, for these are the machinery rather than the Essence of spiritual practice and healing.

The Quality of Healing

The quality of healing depends on the purity of intentions and the level of receptivity.

Poetry is the Language of the Soul

Feelings are the direct expression of the soul. Know the feelings and be with them. This is the strongest communication between soul and mind-body. The soul is the least appreciated aspect of the human being. It is frequently denied, disregarded or rejected. Most of this life, I have been conditioned to deny the existence of soul. With mindful listening, I hear feelings as wisdom whispers through my soul.

I am Nothing

I realize myself as a soul whose chief means of communication is emotion. This soul is partnered with a rational mind whose primary means of communication is human language. The soul and mind manifest along with the physical body which is tangible and concrete, the vehicle for the driver and passenger of this being. "Well, which one am I?" I am three in one. And then, I am nothing at all.

The Silence that we Are

Time for silence, the lull between notes, the pause between
the movements of the symphony when the audience coughs,
and curls are neatly tucked behind our ears in anticipation of
the fiery passage on which the violins are soon to embark. Sit
on the edge of the strings, knowing that we, too, will be
sawed to pieces: the dust of violins, floating gently,
rhythmically to the floor of the orchestral pit to reflect on
what we are: the silence; and the noise: that we are not.

The Anonymous Mind

'Mindfulness' is not the proper term if 'mind' is still considered 'me.' More accurately, we can refer to pure awareness. This does not imply a mind conscious of itself. It does not suggest an entity aware of being. Rather, there is pure Consciousness unattached to this mind or any mind. Consciousness is purely neutral and aware. It is not criticizing, judging or comparing. Awareness means seeing from an anonymous, Universal perspective, a perception of oneness where all exists without division into subject and object, observer and observed.

God's Great Attic

No aspiration to go anywhere. No ambition to accomplish any particular thing. Not lazy, just tinkering in God's great attic and puttering in the garden of the Lord, all of which is me, and yet there is no me. Being is all there is.

Beginning with the Conclusion

How can we observe life from a point of neutrality when we begin our search with a pre-determined conclusion? This strongly conditions the insights that we may discover on our spiritual journey. To meditate while chanting 'no-self, no-self' is a distraction from observing that which is actually occurring at the moment of the meditation. If an 'I' is observed to be breathing during meditation, then observe it. If 'the Universe is breathing,' observe it. If it changes or remains the same, be aware. Monitor the observation process, whoever or whatever it may be. Please do not predetermine what is being observed from a specific belief because that is tantamount to beginning with the conclusion.

Predetermination

To aim for a particular goal during meditation predetermines the 'truth' that will be discovered. That is, to meditate on equanimity or temporality most likely leads to deep faith in those attributes. While these goals may feel good once achieved and could indeed be the ultimate truth, the approach itself demonstrates the fatal epistemological flaw of assuming the conclusion. Employing these pre-selected options distracts us from observing what is truly occurring in the present moment. Is beginning with the 'truth' an epistemologically sound approach to learning?

The Self is a Symptom

The self is important in the same way that cancer is important. The self, like cancer, is a symptom of something deeper within that has grown unchecked. The symptoms provide very important clues into the nature of the life force as it becomes entrenched in a vortex commonly known as self. Self, like cancer, can be described as a repeating pattern of beliefs, attitudes, behaviours, molecular movement, growth and cohesion.

The Evolution of Cancer

Investigating the notion of 'me' is a powerfully heuristic approach. The self is painfully evident to us, because it is a repeating pattern of thoughts and behaviours that are readily identifiable. Those patterns repeat until our personality has been established. It is important to recognize that cancer works in pretty much the same way: Cancer represents a pattern of thought, nutrition or environment that is diseased and out of tune with the life force.

Why Meditate?

The most compelling reason to meditate is the simple wish to meditate, not because we should or must or have to meditate. The most veracious reason to meditate is that you want to meditate. And 'who' is the one that wants to meditate?

The Goal-less Goal

The most legitimate goal of meditating is meditating. No other genuine goal on the agenda can compare. Any expectations are a distraction or predetermination of how the experience will unfurl. Meditation is really quite a goal-less process. Meditate when you want, for as long as you want because you want to meditate in order to meditate. All other rules, reasons or goals serve as foregone conclusions; self-fulfilling prophecies or distractions from unadulterated observation of what genuinely exists.

Negative Vortex

Watch the mind as its primary issues repeat hour after hour of life. For instance, the repeating pattern may be fear: Fear arises, endlessly reciting its theme until it solidifies into a fearful self and reifies into a dangerous material reality. The pattern of emotion or thought indicates the manner in which the energy of the Universal life force is trapped. In this example, fear is spinning in a negative vortex, pulling us further into terror and perpetuating our attachment to self.

Diagnosis of the Universe

To diagnose this pattern, look at fear not only as a personal emotion, but as an entrapment of Universal life energy in a negative holding pattern that ultimately manifests itself as an ulcer, cancer or some other physical malady. To conduct this diagnosis, silently reflect on the emotions, the physical illness and the role of the self. These factors indicate the source of the blockage and the direction towards healing; making whole; the holiness of that being.

Penetrate the Fear

Observe the distress for what it is, as it occurs and repeats.
Monitor the physical manifestation of fear in problems such
as tension or ulcers. Through this process of observation,
awareness of reality awakens. Watch it with steadfast
mindfulness. Observe it whether you like it or not.
Investigate the fear to your deepest roots. Honesty with the
dismay serves a vital function leading you to recognize how
life energy has been trapped in painful emotions.

'Self' is a Blockage in the Universe

The self is important: Not because it is 'me,' but because
'self' indicates a blockage in the Universe. Mindfully observe
the 'self' as it truly operates until you can discern its game
plan, its repetitive nature, until deeper insight into the nature
of self arises. Observe the fear, sadness or anger with
compassion. In terms of healing, this allows the emotion to
dissipate at its own rate. This is the path towards wholeness.
In a sense, healing means to become transparent.

The Nature of our Cure

By working through our angers and pains, and recognizing
these as spiritual symptoms, we gain insight into the nature
of our cure, and also, into the nature of the Universal life
force.

Universal Health

Similarly, observe your present concept of 'self' and
recognize this image as a symptom of how the Universe has
segmented and alienated one branch from the whole. With
this understanding, you gain an opportunity to become
complete. Once intact, you can rest safely beyond self, where
all is one. That is Universal health.

What is the Essence of Wisdom?

The path of wisdom engenders much more than simply
claiming the conclusion. Insight needs to be experienced by
each person on the path. That experience itself is the healing
wisdom. Experience of wisdom is far more important than
cerebral comprehension. Anger and sadness, joy, pain and
fear are sign-posts along the way, indicating the state of the
Universe as it continually manifests.

Here

The Location of Self

Look at self. Where exactly does it begin and end? This air, just centimetres from my nose, is that me? Now the air is in my lungs, has it become me? Soon the oxygen is in my bloodstream pumping through my heart, now is it truly me? Before long, it turns into carbon dioxide, is this also me? Is the air part of myself, or separate? I exhale; the carbon dioxide goes into the garden and is soaked up by a pine tree. Is it still me? Where exactly is the line drawn between what is me and what is not?

Under the Microscope

Look at the skin with a microscope and see trillions of bacteria eating and reproducing everywhere. Every organ of our bodies is host to a million little critters. Are those creatures me? Could I exist without those microscopic beings living together in community? Or, is 'me' only that part that is whole, solid and connected by my personal Consciousness?

Are we One?

But wait a minute. Is the oxygen mentioned a moment ago a part of self or not? If yes, then, trees are my lungs. Similarly, all those microscopic creatures and I must live together or we will cease to exist. Are we one? Our children, our parents, are we one? Our nations and cultures, planets and suns, are we one? If we expand the notion of self to embrace the whole of the Universe, we arrive at the impression that all is one. If that is true, is there still a 'me'?

Who can say 'Me'?

If the whole Universe is one, then only the whole Universe can accurately say 'me.' For the rest of us fragments, we can say, "this present vortex of energy, swirling in this proximity, speaking and eating and hosting these million microscopic creatures, representing the genetic inheritance of millions of generations of other energy vortexes, this, I guess, is me."

Expansive Embrace

Observe the concept of self as it evolves. Observe it
expanding to embrace those around us, our families and
friends. As the notion of self widens, it takes in more and
more, including neighbours, the environment, other living
beings; widening, expanding … how expansive can it
become?

The Arbitrary Self

Once the artificial boundaries of 'self' are perceived as being
arbitrary and highly permeable, the notion of self can be
surrendered.

Self is then experienced as an illogical belief that is highly
permeable and malleable. Proceed along this course until all
boundaries are dissolved and self merges with the whole.

Exegesis of the Universe

These explorations of the Universe are not simply exercises in semantics. Using human vernacular to describe experiences that don't make sense in rational language is quite the challenge. The insights and observations shared within these pages are not of an intellectual nature, even if the whole reading feels cerebral. If it were all so easy as to merely 'click here' to know.

Exploring the Source of Anger

It has been puzzling and torturing me to meditate these many months, watching myself foaming at the mouth with anger. I've observed myself angry at everybody and everything, pointing fingers and picking fights, blaming and criticizing and condemning every person, place and thing within the reach of my venom. I have chronicled the anger and documented the hatred. My meditation has taken various turns, blacker and darker and angrier. The anger never really changed character although I watched it diligently under the scrutiny of mindfulness. Somehow, mindfulness was sabotaged and turned into self-consciousness. Finally, I apprehended that I hated that I hated and I was angry that I was angry. I had achieved the perfection of self-sabotage. And then…

The Ultimate Source of Health

…yesterday the anger broke. It fizzled out and finally passed after nearly a year of intense observation. It was not a particularly happy year, busy as I was with hating the Universe and every being that resides in it. The truth perceived was that I hated myself so deeply, and was so disgusted and disappointed in myself, that I hated and blamed everybody else to ease the pain. The emotional illness was the key to deconstructing my illusions. Eventually, I began to experience inner peace. The turning point was triggered by reading that illness is the degree to which our lives are out of synch with our true natures. Thus, to know and be our true selves is the ultimate source of good health.

Projection for Protection

Are all the things that I despise and fear actually projections
of my own caustic inner self? Do you mean that it is more
convenient for me to hate and blame others than to admit
my inner enmity?

Toxic Environment

Does this imply that all the rubbish that I see in politics,
economics, culture and society, business and corporations,
cities and states, pollution, congestion, wastes and chemical-
warfare are the toxins of the inner organs of the dark inner
being, of which I have no cognition? The piercing stab is
realizing that my social critiques are projections of the inner
lambasting that I perpetuate against myself.

Like

For decades, I never allowed myself to like or approve of myself. One day, I disembarked from that emotional bus and there I was in the present moment, enjoying being me and being with myself. The only 'like' that truly matters is that I like myself.

Self Ceases to be an Individual

Ironically, learning to accept and like myself greatly empowers me to loosen my grip on the notion of self. Since I am no longer so desperately defending my weak spirit against criticism, I can easily open my heart. By opening my heart, the sense of 'self' rapidly expands to include more and more people. Self ceases to be an individual me. It becomes an open, porous, spontaneously evolving 'whole self' that comprises the greater world.

Sabotage of the Soul

Do I actively deny my soul its ontological status? Does this sabotage spiritual liberation?

Inside the Silence

The only thing to be done is reckoning with the inner silence and peering into the vast internal emptiness. In such throes, perceive that silence is infinitely deeper and emptier than conceived at the outset. Inside, entrenched in the labyrinths of the human heart, the encounter with the barrenness of the ego-self awaits.

Treadmill of the Ego

As David Hawkins has explained, the time between a thought taking place and the ego claiming ownership is about one ten-thousandth of a second. Consequently, we need to get our mindfulness up to speed, quicker than the ego's imperial pursuits. High-speed wi-fi mindfulness is required to recognize the futility of our myriad pursuits: from organizing the icons on our desktops to painting the office walls. Other times, we engross ourselves in seeking a guru, traveling the world or saving it from itself. These are all manifestations of the treadmill of the ego trying to prove the reality and importance of its existence. The ego deceives us into believing its perpetually spinning yarns.

Spiritual Straightjacket

The ego exists, in its own convoluted way, but that is not you. It's more like a jacket that keeps you warm in the winter, but suffocates you during the springtime of your spiritual blossoming. Eventually, the unchallenged ego-self hardens into a straightjacket from which it becomes increasingly difficult to extricate the soul.

Exploring Silence

The cessation of running, the quiet fortitude of exhaustion as it blankets the city with despair. The authentic being awaits the courage to sit in front of the blank page at the empty desk in the vacuous room on the deserted planes in order to dwell with the boredom. Fatigued by the frustration and the fight, only the courage to be bored remains. Explore silence, blank and dull. Admire the empty slate. Avoid the compulsion to fill in all of the spaces. Be there.

Unremitting Distractions

Sit in meditation like a lotus and be bored, sore, stiff or
stressed. Do not resist or try to escape. Any of a thousand
emotions may arise as part of the blossoming process. Please
don't get busy with chores and run away. This is it. With
patience, persistence and acceptance, mindfulness takes the
upper hand and the barriers that prevent insight wither away.
The mechanizations of the ego gradually weaken and the
perpetual distractions that were constructed to avoid
confrontation with the void progressively fade.

Silence Soothes the Sores

Sitting in silent meditation is no career; there are no medals.
It may not be musical, sexy or savoury. It is empty; it does
not make the news and you can hardly boast to your
colleagues about it. You can only sit and be bored until the
restlessness, the struggle and resistance gradually weaken,
allowing you to succumb to the bliss. Eventually all of the
nasty stuff dissolves, and silence permeates the stage. Inner
peace is the salve that soothes the sores of the injured ego as
it comes to terms with its own deception, face to face with
its own expiration date.

The Great Escape

But what happens next? Distraction! Give me anything to escape this mute introspection. Make coffee, clean the windows, go for lunch, another coffee, sink into the compulsions of activity that boost the sense that there is a real individual me-myself-I with a purpose and a point, all pulling me further into the world of distraction that I perceive, conceive and perpetuate.

Mind You

That world that we perceive is a projection put forth by the ludicrous ego-self. This world that we create-project is a figment of the ego's obsessive-compulsive frantically busy, maniacally possessive and needy character. The external world is the sum total of feelings and expectations from the inner world projected onto the blank screen of the raw Universe, and then, coyly, naively, supposedly, perceived! Secure silence and get down to the truth.

Thoughts Thinking

We are not thinking any of this. There is no you or me that is
thinking. Thoughts, ideas and opinions are thinking us!
Consequently, they are perpetuating the sense of self. Be
silent, relax and smile at the illusions. The ideas and beliefs
that arise in your mind are not synonymous with who you
truly are. With awareness, observe these mental phenomena
as they struggle for your attention and pilfer your serenity.
Therein resides the Essence.

The Essence of Healing

Healing depends on what we are prepared to release. The
illnesses and injuries that each person holds onto represent
the armour of an unhealthy notion of self.

Diagnosis of the Soul

What do our social attitudes and political opinions reveal
about our spiritual evolution? How can we diagnose our
souls through analysis of our poetry and politics?

Reverse Engineering the Soul

Can you reverse-engineer the soul through analysis of the
social attitudes that you broadcast?

Humility or Ego

To what degree do our thoughts benefit or harm humanity?
Do our actions nurture or threaten others? Does our
behaviour propagate humility or ego?

Simmering Neurosis

Personality consists of an insistent flow of neurotic thoughts
establishing recognizable and predictable patterns of
behaviour and attitudes, culminating in what we mistakenly
consider to be the self. These thoughts simmer in the subconscious below the level of awareness. Thoughts arise to
the conscious level so quickly and with such familiarity as to
remain undetected by the average mind untrained in the
endeavour of mindfulness. Thoughts establish such
repetitive patterns of behaviour and belief so as to create the
illusion of a self: a 'me' who experiences the pattern and
claims ownership of that identity.

Appreciation

We don't need to believe Newton's laws of gravity in order
to appreciate the joy of lying on a grassy lawn.

The Self is merely an App

The unspoken ideology of individual self creates a paradigm
in which me-myself-and-I are supreme. The self is
unconsciously perpetuated by thought. The self exists
because of the application of a paradigm of self. The
paradigm creates the self. In the absence of thought,
language, reason and explanation, the self disappears because
it is merely a function of those tools.

Existential Pond

The self is as provisional as a pond: remove the banks of the
pond and the pond ceases to exist. Similarly, remove the
paradigm (the construct of language and thought) of 'self'
and the self ceases to exist. The self only exists within the
paradigm, just as the pond exists only within the banks. The
banks of the pond and the paradigm of self are both
provisional structures.

The Ego is but a Wave

A wave on the ocean is an event, rather than an object. It exists temporally and phenomenologically. Similarly, the self is an event, not an object. It occurs in place and time, but lacks authentic ontology. Who knows this? Awareness knows.

We are the Ponds of the Universe

When all the water in a pond evaporates during the hot summer months, the pond ceases to exist. It returns to nature and blends in with the other elements – air, earth and fire. The pond was temporal – an event in time and space more so than presenting a definite ontologically confirmed reality. We are thus.

Self-Contradiction

How can the self seek to understand non-self? That is a contradiction in terms.

The 'self' is not seeking to understand itself. It would be more accurate to understand that Consciousness is exploring the Universe via the lens of the individual human mind.

The Essence of the Universe is Awareness

Who is aware? Awareness is nature in the same way that gravity is nature. These forces simply exist. You do not need a subject to activate gravity any more than you need a subject to activate awareness. Awareness is an inherent characteristic of the Universe.

Our Quantum Existence

The wave – does it exist? Capture a wave in a bucket, and where is the wave? It has ceased to exist. A wave is an event, just as 'self' is an event. The self is a concurrence of phenomena at the material and conscious levels, held together long enough to appear solid and real. If you consider an object to be solid, this equates to a particle in quantum physics. Conversely, the self is more like a quantum wave. When you contemplate the self as a wave, you will apprehend it as a wave. This is a portrait of our quantum existence.

When the Self Evaporates

When the mind is silent, when language and reason are
nought, when explanation is avoided, the 'self' evaporates
like a pond in summer or like a wave crashing on the shores
of non-existence. The self evaporates, or implodes, and the
'non-self' becomes apparent. Actually, the 'non-self' can be
more accurately defined as Universal awareness. Eternal
awareness, as the Essence of the Universe, is ever present. It
is not cerebrally knowable when inspected through the veil
of the ego.

Puddles of Insight

The ego cannot truly fathom non-self. Ego vainly believes
that it understands. This further prevents comprehension.
This is like a puddle refusing to evaporate in summer and
declining to synthesize into the atmosphere in order to once
again fall as rain and become one with the ocean. The puddle
tenaciously hangs onto its 'puddle-ness' just as the human
hangs onto 'me-ness.' The puddle and the pond, the ocean
and the self, are all one and the same thing, except for the
artificial borders and concepts that keep them separate.

Duality

To give a thing a name reinforces the duality between the item and its observer. This duality divides the world into us and them, object and subject, flower and weed. To name a thing is to separate yourself from it.

The Wildflower

The aim of the wildflower
Is to remain unnamed

Persecution

But look! The poem itself is named. The wildflower has successfully escaped the shackles of a title, but the poem about the wildflower continues to abide by convention. The poem has betrayed its own sovereignty.

Where is the Essence?

Essence resides beyond practice, symbols, concepts, and even beyond comprehension. Maintain awareness of this Essence by consciously breathing it in with every breath. The Essence truly has no label or name. It lacks identity, yet it is all there is. You might give it a name, but that name is nothing but a handle, a symbol or a label. Please do not mistake the label for the Essence itself. The Essence can be discussed, explained, symbolized and reified, but it remains ineffable.

Tune in to the Universe

Be aware of the false dichotomy between you and the
Universe. You are a part of the Universe, and, you are the
whole Universe. Maintain this awareness.

'Who' is Thinking?

In seeking to understand the Consciousness of the Universe,
I've come to question, 'who' is thinking? Who is asking and
wondering? Is it the Universe thinking, asking and
observing? Or, are these actions without actors, verbs
without nouns? Just as gravity pulls without a puller, the
Universe thinks without a thinker and wonders without a
wonderer. This is the natural Essence of the Universe.

Blaming is Claiming

When I blame others, it's like I'm claiming them as my own,
as if they must follow me and meet my standards. I blame
'them' but it's truly me blaming myself. This understanding
leads to compassion: It makes sense to be compassionate
with others, especially when we realize that, effectively, they
are projections or extensions of ourselves. When we register
critical or judgmental thoughts in the mind… transform
them into compassion for the victims of those thoughts.

Criticism is Projection

Criticism is a projection of inner anger or pain. Projecting it
onto others seems like a release, but actually, it is just blame.
This is violence at a subtle psychological level. Criticism of
others reveals a great deal about ourselves. Anger in the
mind is violence towards all. Take a deep, therapeutic breath
every time you recognize blame or criticism rising into mind.
During the duration of the breath, consciously convert the
blame into compassion for others and compassion for self.

The Creations of Mind

We each have access to some aspect of totality and we claim this to be reality. Our belief in our perceived aspects is so strong and solid that it becomes real. It becomes concrete. It becomes objective. So powerful, so creative is mind that it creates and produces reality / objectivity.

Collective Realities

Collectively, we create the totality, the Universe. The Universe is a collection of diverse realities. Each 'reality' is complete in itself, yet it is only one aspect of the totality. One reality does not exclude another: multiple realities exist within the totality.

Diverse Truths

Totality is so complete that it engenders diverse and
paradoxical realities within it. There are no contradictions
because the totality, the Universe, is not a single truth.
Rather, it is a collective of all aspects of diverse 'truths.' The
Universe is not necessarily logical; why would it be
constrained by human rationality?

Belief is a Concrete Alchemical Process

I used to think that objectification was an academic or social
process whereby subjective opinions took on objective
status. Now I see that objectification is far more powerful
than I had imagined. Objectification is the concrete,
alchemical metamorphosis from one level of ontological
status to another. Namely, mental belief becomes solidified
in material reality. That reality becomes valid not only for the
one who has objectified it, but it becomes an objective
aspect of the Universe. Each 'objectified' creation is just as
real as its opposite.

Paradox is the Nature of the Universe

The God-Universe engenders opposites and paradoxes as its
natural course.

Thought Literally Creates

Thought creates material reality. Belief not only evaluates, it
also creates and produces. Belief and thought collectively
create the world as we believe / think it to be. You've heard
this before: As you sow, so shall you reap. It's true, literally,
on a colossal scale. We create / project the society in which
we live, which concurrently creates / produces its people and
its events. Reciprocal creation and causation produce and
perpetuate the world and its Consciousness.

Sentience

Every living being is conscious – feeling – sentient. Please be
continually and Universally aware of this.

A Question of Rights

Which animals do humans have a right to kill?

Gift

I have only my presence to offer you, in equal exchange for
your presence. You are my gift and I am yours.

God

God both exists and does not exist.

Beyond Limitations

God as conceived by most humans is limited by personification, culture, religion and history. The concept of God is further constrained by thought, language, ideology, science and philosophy.

God is beyond all such limitations. God is beyond all attributes. God is beyond time and space.

All of this said, God neither exists nor does not exist.

Do I Exist?

I both exist and do not exist. I neither exist nor do not exist.

Pure Essence

All is pure phenomena, pure energy, in the absence of any
distinction between self and non-self. The realm of pure
energy / bare awareness / raw Consciousness / Essence
resides in the absence of any distinction between God and
no God; between self and non-self; between God and self;
between self and nature.

Thought Obfuscates Reality

This thought inclusive.

Who Meditates Whom?

Universal Consciousness meditates you, more so than you meditate on Consciousness. One segment of the Universe is contemplating its fragmentation from the whole.

What is Self?

Self is a fragment of the Universe. It is also a holograph of the Universe. The self is nothingness; and, it is the Universe replete.

Meditation is Unification

Who or what is meditation for? Meditation is unification
with one-ness, with Universal Consciousness.

Compensation for Blindness

Be careful not to inflate your religiosity to compensate for a
relative dearth of spirit. Sadly, religion can often be the
greatest hindrance to spirituality. Attachment to doctrine can
cause blindness to Essence. A strong focus on form can
cause deafness to spirit.

Necessary and Fatal

The ego is a necessary and essential aspect for the very
survival of a being. It is both necessary, and fatal, to
evolution.

Entanglement

'Self' and 'non-self' constitute a false dichotomy. These are not opposites. Rather, 'self' can be thought of as the provisional individual ego that provides initial identity for social and physical survival. 'Non-self'' may be more effectively termed 'Universal Consciousness' that expresses itself through a wide array of voices and guises. Universal Consciousness has become deeply entangled in its 'receiver-projector' individuals and finds this state grossly binding. Once the entanglement is recognized, the Universe may extricate itself from individual identification and proceed with shining its light.

Nature Seeking Itself

This life is the very quest of nature exploring and discovering itself.

Validation Disempowers

As long as we seek validation, we remain disempowered.

What is Consciousness?

The Universe is the source of human intelligence. The
Universe is conscious and intelligent more so than it is
material. The Universe is Consciousness itself. The Universe
is not just a bunch of rocks, carbon and atoms. Rather, it is a
conscious, feeling, thinking organism. Oddly, people claim
ontological status for our human egos but deny it to the very
source of our Consciousness. Once we see that the Universe
is conscious, we no longer query how human Consciousness
could have evolved from mere inorganic atoms.

From a Thought to an Earthquake

Everything is an energy exchange, from a thought, to an earthquake, to admiring the leaves on a tree. The Universe 'is' energy, rather than 'has' energy. Be aware of the importance of this distinction. Energy is the Essence of the Universe. We could call this energy the life force itself. Reiki is not a 'healing energy' per se. Rather, the technique of Reiki is the focusing of the Universal life force towards healing purposes. Using Reiki entails directing life force towards therapeutic ends.

Deference to the Universe

By entering deep meditation with three very wilful breaths, the me-myself-I consciousness fades. Universal Consciousness is willed into presence by deference of the individuated self to the Universe.

The Universe is Conscious

The Universe is energy; it is conscious. It has gravity and centripetal force. All of these are its natural characteristics. The Universe is intelligent and aware as proven by its human participants, its playful squirrels, its sparrows and wrens, among numerous other beings.

The Essence of Every Being

If you love animals… why do you eat them?

You may love cats and dogs, which shows kindness and compassion. But, do you request that pigs or chickens be killed for your lunch? Pigs, chickens, cows and ducks care about their babies just as much as dogs love their puppies. All animals have feelings and experience joy, companionship, fear and pain. They love life just as much as you love life. That is the Essence of every being. Every time you eat meat, the life of one animal must be stolen. Who is ultimately responsible?

What is Reiki?

Reiki is the Essence of the Universe. Reiki is not merely a force or energy in the Universe. Rather, Reiki is the Universe incarnate. To use Reiki implies focused volition and consciously tuning into the greater whole, the Universe / Consciousness. The process of Reiki involves knowing at a visceral level that all is energy, and behaving in a manner consistent with this innate knowledge.

Reiki is a Smile

Reiki is a smile, the gentle caress of a butterfly, the kindness of words. All are Reiki; all of these events are subtle exchanges of energy.

Is the God-Universe Conscious?

Universal and Consciousness are two characteristics suggested by the concept of 'God.' No separation exists between 'my' Consciousness, 'Universal' Consciousness and 'God' Consciousness. One holographically engenders the others. The 'I' is merely an arbitrary division of some aspect of totality into an individualized, personified entity.

God makes the Universe Comprehensible

God is an anthropomorphic representation of the conscious
Universe. The term 'God' makes the Universe
understandable at a human level. Humans often relate to a
personified 'being' more concretely than abstract Essence.
Experience of one-ness makes this more clear. It may be
helpful to think of one-ness as in the Sufi's swirling to unite
with God. The Sufis dance in a frenzy until the self dissolves
and only God remains.

'Who' is Meditating?

First, let's respond with a counter-question: "Is there a
meditator?" The question, "Who is meditating?" assumes
some entity is taking action. Actually, meditation takes place
without necessarily having a 'who' performing it.

Is meditation a natural characteristic of Universal
Consciousness?

Introspection and reflection are inherent characteristics of
the Universe. The Universe is aware of itself. Reflection is
accomplished through conscious minds.

'Who' is Asking?

Are questions that arise concerning 'who' posed by an ontological being? Or, are these questions naturally arising within the Universe in search of itself? Who is meditating?

The alienated self is seeking unity with wholeness. The inherent wisdom of the Universe that resides within the individuated self is meditating, regardless of the individual's delusional identity.

Sentient Reflections

Living beings enable the Universe to reflect on itself. In so doing, the Universe evolves. It perceives itself through the eyes, nose, ears and souls of its sentient beings.

'I' Disappears

Meditation is not just for you. It's for the whole Universe.
With meditation by the Universe, for the Universe, the 'I'
disappears.

During Meditation, 'Who' is Aware?

Experience at this level of Universal awareness indicates that
it's not 'me' that is aware. Rather, it's the Universe itself that
is aware. Similarly, the perception arises that it is not 'me'
that is breathing, but the Universe itself that is breathing.
When the entire 'me' becomes silent, all actions, perceptions
and awareness are recognized as being Universal in nature.

What is the Origin of the Self?

The ego-self is fragmented from the whole specifically because of the construct of self. Materially, at the atomic or elemental level, the human body is identical to the rest of the Universe. The concepts of self and self-preservation prevent the fragment from returning to the meld. The concept of the self separates 'I' from 'Universe.' Without that concept separating us, it is readily apparent that we ARE the Universe. We are manifestations of the intelligence of the Universe.

Does the Universe realize that it Exists?

Yes, the Universe knows that it exists, and knows it from within the whole as well as its splintered parts. This is why squirrels on a Sunday morning at Acacia Park can be seen dancing, diving, delving, chasing, cheering, popping, poking and peering with their mates with as much enthusiasm as a five-man-band covering old Eagles' tunes, and they do it, the squirrels, not for the money or the fame, but just because they are, and they can, and they do, and they exist, and they love life. The squirrels are the Universe at play. The Universe plays!

Silence is the Deepest Liberation

Why does it seem impossible for people of different religions or political perspectives to communicate?

Mainly, it's due to paradigmatic constipation and epistemological castration. We get trapped in our own perspectives and paradigms, denying alternative ways of understanding and experiencing the Universe. Our very approach towards truth or God is inherently castrated. Silence is the deepest liberation from these constraints.

Absolute Permeability

Surrender is the greatest path to inner victory. Surrender has nothing to do with giving up or with losing. Surrender is entirely concerned with opening the heart-mind-soul to a state of absolute permeability.

Ontological Fear

Recognizing several dimensions of anger / fear can be insightful. Operational anger arises in daily situations. It is fuelled by much deeper existential anger, which is the barking of a frightened dog. The barking allays the much deeper existential fear at the core of its being. This includes fear of abandonment, being alone in life or being alone in the Universe. Ontological fear is the fear of not actually existing, which is a very valid fear because the self does not ontologically exist. It is merely a very pervasive and persuasive illusion.

The Split from the Whole

How did the ego split off from the Universal whole?

It is within the potential of the Universe to splinter itself. The individuated parts get 'lost' by dismissing the splintering and then hopelessly believing in the illusion of an individuated self. Keep aware that the ego-self is an indiscriminate division, as arbitrary as national borders that divide up a continent. Ego-self is merely a mental construct that perpetuates distraction and delusion, but has no material reality.

Let it Fade Away

How can we return to the whole (Universe, health, enlightenment)?

We need to stop reinforcing the ego and let it fade away. The ego-self is self-preserving and this perpetuates the separatism. Allow the ego to be injured and then observe the pain without reacting. Reaction is the re-assertion of the primacy of the ego-self. Non-reaction is the surrender of the illusion of self… into wholeness and health.

Why does the Ego Persist?

The ego struggles to maintain the illusion of a self through
all possible means such as opinions and accomplishments.
Each time you recognize these factors attempting to
sabotage wholeness, take a long deep breath.

The deep breath helps unplug the grandiosity of the ego.
The ego struggles to allay existential fear, to deny and
suppress the fear that it (the ego-self) does not actually exist.
The self is merely a concept. Once you permit all of this,
experientially, you cease to exist, 'you' return to one-ness.

Maintain Presence

How can we maintain presence in the Universal
Consciousness?

The Universe is breathing, thinking, meditating, looking and
listening. Keep this in mind when a meditator gets drawn
into human thought, which greatly narrows and skews
Universal intelligence. Maintain awareness of the Universe
breathing and observing. Make this a conscious, determined
effort. Remain equanimous and neutral so as to not distort
the Universe's perspective of itself. Preserve silence, inside
and out. Avoid being defensive because that would clearly be
an ego action.

Synchronize with One-ness

Synchronize the mind and actions of the individuated self
with the natural one-ness of the Universe. This brings the
former into the whole by gradually dissolving the ego.
Encourage a positive dissolution by promising a far greater
existence as one-ness.

Nature's Mindfulness

When we attain a certain level of concentration and
mindfulness, ego-chatter becomes quieter. In this silence,
mindfulness arises, comprising a wider awareness of the
body, of the surroundings, and an awareness of deeper
intelligence. This is Universal awareness: nature's
mindfulness.

Perception without Judgment

Recent experience shows that the Universe is not judgmental. It perceives, it is aware, it observes. There is no need to judge people or things because the Universe is already at peace. It is equanimous with all things in this world.

Conversely, when the ego-mind is self-conscious, a great deal of judgment arises. This frequently manifests as negative judgment concerning the perceived faults in other people. This negative judgment confirms the self-interest of the ego-mind and its need to condemn others in order to feel good about itself. Low self-esteem makes this ego-mind even harsher than usual.

Raw Potential

What is the human relationship to reality?

We, as participants in the Universe, project our beliefs, ideas
and concepts onto the 'raw potential' of the Universe. This
leads us to 'perceive' reality, which is actually our projection.
Then we interpret the perception, which really means to
objectify things and to transform concepts into objects. We
do all of this in accordance with our pre-defined paradigms
and concepts. Our interpretations then confirm our original
concepts, as in a self-fulfilling prophecy. The process of
projection-perception-objectification-interpretation fails to
prove anything concerning the existence of an *a priori*
objective Universe.

Creators of the World

The Universe is 'created' or 'activated' by its observers /
participants. Each one of us is creating a world that
conforms to our own beliefs. This is why everybody is
always right! Everybody creates the Universe. We all
interpret the Universe and call this being objective. It might
be better to call it being 'paradigmatically objective' or
'religiously objective' or, better yet, 'subjectively objective.'

How is the Universe 'Created'?

We are creators – each of us – in our thoughts – create every
situation – every event. Humans emerge from a source of
raw potential, actualizing through action and experience. It is
helpful to ask yourself in a given situation, 'am I projecting
or perceiving; am I creating or observing?'

Leap into Actuality

The raw potential of the Universe is always already present,
ready to 'leap' into 'actuality.' The Universe actualizes in the
moment that a person begins to believe that something
exists in a particular way. The actuality thus initiated
becomes a material reality that is consistent with the
adherents of that belief. The actualization consequently
confirms the perspective of the adherents that created it
through their collective beliefs. Usually, a belief is
unassailable from outside that perspective because the ego is
so grandiosely self-protective that it literally creates a
physical world in order to justify its own beliefs.

The Universe Gladly Obliges

Do we prove what we already believe, or do we believe what
we have proven?

Both a believer in a flat earth and a believer in a spherical
earth will prove everything according to their perspective.
They will deny or disprove everything contrary to their view.
The world gladly obliges by shaping itself to each respective
belief. If you refuse to believe this, the Universe adapts to
your beliefs and makes it false. If you think this paradoxical
explanation is crazy, then it's crazy. If you think it's
profound, it's profound. If you think it's profoundly crazy…

Beyond Rational Thought

The Universe is so infinitely beyond rational human thought that it can hold numerous mutual contradictions in its womb. The earth is both flat and round; it is neither flat nor round, it is all of these, and none of these. The earth more resembles a system of thought than a material planet.

Infinite Possibility

Is there any absolute reality to the Universe?

The Universe is a raw potential field of infinite possibility and eternal manifestations of intelligence. The Universe affords itself to diverse, simultaneous and contradictory actualizations. For example, a physicist experiences particles and waves; a healer feels Reiki; a shaman communicates with gnomes and elves; a Christian has faith in Jesus and angels; while an atheist materialist accepts nothing except empirical matter. Collectively, these views create a Universe with the respective characteristics that are produced by the perceivers-creators themselves. The true creators of the Universe are its participants who create it through projection of their beliefs. The Universe does not simply exist *a priori* and then we perceive it. Rather, we conceive-create it and then it actualizes.

Quiet beyond Thought

What is the nature of thought?

Thought is a natural characteristic of this intelligent Universe. The challenge is to experience this point when functioning within the constraints of ego-thought. Remaining quiet beyond thought makes it easier to encounter the non-personal nature of intelligence.

How does the Universe Perceive?

The Universe perceives through the eyes of its creatures. The Universe is self-reflective, peering through the eyes of every sentient being in the Universe. The Universe hears itself through the ears of its life forms. Creatures are the sensory organs of the Universe. Mobility is an important factor here. Kinetic creatures provide vital bio-feedback to the Universe for monitoring and adjustment.

Actualizing Essence

Should we just observe or should we actualize ourselves as active creators?

We know that thought influences matter. We recognize that thought is Universal Consciousness. We have experienced that mindfulness is Universal awareness. Now we apprehend that this ego-self fragment of the Universe through which the Universe meditates upon itself can passively observe and know itself and /or purposefully create and evolve itself, with no preference or bias towards one or the other. To merely observe phenomena denies the creative / actualizing Essence of the Universal mind. 'Mere observation' denies the literally creative aspect of intelligence.

Universally Present

Be the life force. Open all the doors and windows of the world and be Universally present.

Humility

I hope that through humility I can experience pure Essence
by surrendering to nature.

Surrender

Surrender to the Universe.

Mutual Tuning

Consciously tune / adjust / adapt to the Universe. Request
the Universe to adapt / adjust / tune into you. Mutual
tuning and merging from both dimensions leads to
wholeness.

Universal Sovereignty

Cede personal sovereignty only to the Universe and never to any institution or organization, any entity, leader, teacher, doctrine or dogma. Blend personal sovereignty into Universal sovereignty.

Co-Healing

I consciously tune and adapt my heart to the truth of the Universe. I am true to the Universe and the Universe is true to me. This harmony is the Essence of health.

Happiness is an Inside Job

I know that happiness is always an inner task, yet I continue to expect others to please me, respect me, be interested in me and support me.

Identification with Thoughts

Thought is a natural and impersonal characteristic of the
Universe, yet I continue to identify the thoughts as my own.
I even believe that I am the thoughts. I even create my
identity based on thoughts. This grand duality diverts me
from wholeness.

Effortless Being

I know that pure being is the true path, yet I continue to
conceptualize ways of trying 'being' rather than just being.
'Trying to be' is, in itself, a barrier to true being. This is why
true meditation, like pure being, is totally effortless.

The Limits of Form

Employ spiritual or esoteric forms, techniques and methods
only to the extent that these lead you towards Essence. More
than that and you may become attached to form, posture or
external manifestations of the discipline. Less than that and
you may remain indifferent to Essence for lack of clarity and
precision.

Allow Nature to be Happy

Nature effortlessly observes and feels its own breath.

Nature's Contentment

Being true to your heart is nature's contentment.

Happiness is the Cause

Happiness is the cause of a good day, more so than the result of a good day. Happiness is the source more than the consequence. Happiness is a conscious choice. Be conscious of it.

Anger and Sadness are Options

Nature is angry -
Honour that anger
Without owning it

Nature is sad -
Respect that sadness
Without buying it

Nature is fear -
Recognize that fear
Without bringing it home

In the Absence

In the absence of distractions and delusions, in the absence
of calendars and phones, resides the silent Essence.

God is the Ideal Projection

'God' is the ideal projection of what we think / feel / believe life should be at the highest, divine level of being.

Waves of Thought

Observe the thinking… but is there a thinker? A continuum of thought pervades the Universe. Indeed, thought is the long and short of the Universe. Matter (particles) in the Universe is only incidental. Thus, 'my' thoughts are actually waves of Universal thought. They are ebbing and flowing with a particular pattern that has come to be known as me. This 'me' is nothing more than a pattern of behaviour or a series of actions.

Essence Is

Yoga is invisible; it slightly concerns the body. Mantra is silent; it just barely concerns sound. Reiki is heart; and scarcely concerns the hands. Essence is.

Proceed into Essence

Please transcend postures and symbols, scriptures and
visions, beliefs and cultures, religions and dogmas. Proceed
into Essence: it is naturally holistic and holistically natural.
Essence is ineffable; it is one. When we are in Essence, we
have no need to discuss how we arrived.

Only Presence

I long believed that one-ness implied bridges spanning the
world to make connections. Now I understand that family,
students and friends are already essential aspects of me.
There is no absence, only presence. Bridges are not required
to traverse what is already one.

Waiting for Rain

A prophet on top of the mountain waits for rain to wash his
words away.

The Vanity of Ultimate Truth

There is some odd comfort in thinking that we know the monumental absolute truths of God and the Universe. Too often, this is mere vanity. Not knowing requires a lot more courage. Lack of knowledge is a primal motivation for seeking, exploring, creating and imagining our Essence. This pries open the heart-mind-soul of the Universe.

Wholeness is the Essence of Health

Wholeness is the Essence of health. Neurotic standards of hygiene are the most serious threat to strong immunity. The most likely place to acquire disease is at hospital. Meanwhile, one of the greatest distractions from true health comes from belief in insurance. Wholeness is an internal process that marginally depends on medical institutions.

That which only Seekers Find

Too often, we become blinded by religion, deafened by sermons and numbed by scripture. Please recall what the Sufis have taught: The thing of which we speak can never be found by seeking, yet only seekers find it.

Here

Entangled in Form

To be entangled in form is to strangle Essence.

Irrationality

The most irrational belief is the notion that we are rational
beings.

Woe

Belief in objectivity is a woefully subjective perspective.

True to the Universe

When you are true to yourself, you are true to the Universe.
Finally, you experience that there is no 'self' distinct from the
Universe.

The Labyrinth

Years and years of exploring the labyrinths of his soul, he
recognizes the Universe… As many years pondering the vast
reaches of the cosmos, has led him to apprehend his soul. In
one flash, the big-bang of Consciousness burst… and he
experienced the Universe within his soul.

A Unique Contribution

Each human perspective is a unique contribution to multi-
dimensional subjective reality, rather than a distortion of
some supposed objective reality.

Perpetual Flux

A static historical dogma cannot keep us in tune with a God-
Universe-self that is in perpetual flux.

Without Abdication

Surrender the individual self. Silence personal thought. Dissolve identity. But do not abdicate responsibility as you metamorphosize into the Universal life force of divine will.

Honour the Life Force

Please honour the life force within you, within all people, as it manifests. Please respect what people are, rather than what you think they should be. Please revere the life force within all beings. Please do not steal the force of life from any sentient being. Please.

Religious Bully

Why do we have to be the best? A deep need to be the greatest and to dominate others is nothing more than entrenched insecurity and inferiority. This is characteristic of a bully-nation or bully-religion that dominates others in order to compensate for sub-conscious inferiority and insecurity.

Be the Light!

Don't just visualize, don't just think, but consciously radiate positive, whole loving light. Light is the essential element. Be the light of life, the light of love, effortlessly, for this is what we naturally are.

Here to be Human

You are here to be human, while retaining spiritual Essence. You are a spiritual-human being, which is a redundancy, because human in itself engenders spirit. It's only in empirical thought that the notion of 'human' denies spirit and emphasizes biology.

Beyond Comprehension

Universal Consciousness is far beyond intelligence. It can be abstracted and portrayed as saints or sages, angels or gods. Yet, this process of personification leads to reductionism, distorting the whole that continues to elude comprehension.

Strength

True strength is patience, allows weakness, and seeks
support.

Be Ubiquitous

Be infinite. Be eternal. Be ubiquitous. This is what we are.
Allow ubiquity to flow through this being for perfect health
and alignment with life. Prophets, guides, gods and angels
remain limited by their conceptual, institutional, cultural,
material or anthropomorphic straight-jackets. Liberate
yourself and be.

What is Ubiquity?

Ubiquity refers to that which transcends, and includes, all…
without giving it a name. It remains nebulous without being
constrained by a physical concept that implies location, or
mental concepts that masquerade as comprehension.

What is the Incarnate Truth?

Teachings concerning the truth are not the truth incarnate.
The incarnate truth transcends any words or language,
definition or interpretation, explanation or analysis,
comprehension or belief. The incarnate truth transcends all,
eclipsing even this transcendence.

You can only Be the Truth

The scriptures are not the truth. The teacher is not the truth. Our understanding is not the truth. The truth is beyond all such limitations. Experience truth without using language, scripture, belief or thought. Truth concerns being; it does not concern knowing. You cannot know the truth. You can only be the truth.

Presence

Are Essence and presence one and the same?

Visceral Experience of Raw Truth

Can we encounter raw experience without employing interpretation, language, teaching, understanding and wisdom? Raw experience yields '   '. Conversely, ideas, knowledge and concepts merely refer to truth. These notions are already one step removed from truth due to the dualistic nature of language and thought. The solution? Visceral experience of raw truth.

What is the Essence of Happiness?

Happiness is your unconditional decision. It is a choice that you make independent of people, conditions or situations.

Disempowerment

You are disempowered any time you want somebody to
show interest in you. When you are interested in yourself,
and approve of yourself, this is sufficient cause for
contentment.

What is the Essence of Moods?

We may not wake up and consciously choose to be angry or
depressed on a given day. Yet, at a deeper level, we have
chosen anger or sadness because these moods satisfy our
desire for pity, admiration or love. Look deep within to
observe the reality of these emotional decisions. Are these
the emotions of the ego or of the soul?

Proper Attire

Observe the mood in which you attire yourself each day.
Your mood fashions the day.

Passengers on a Whim

When we allow our moods to respond to events, we are
mere passengers, dependent on the whims of external factors
for our well-being.

Happiness is the Primal Source

Can we wait for other people to make us happy? That would
make happiness the result of life events. More effectively, we
can choose inner, unconditioned happiness as the primal
source of ensuing events.

What is Enlightenment?

Enlightenment is your choice. It is the cause of
understanding and compassion, as much as the result of
understanding and compassion. I choose to be enlightened. I
choose how to define this and I choose how to live it.
Enlightenment is not a Yogi thing or a religious thing or a
meditation thing; it is your own thing.

To think that enlightenment is an objective state as defined
by a teacher or a text is highly constraining. Those
definitions are culturally emasculated and historically static.
It makes infinitely more sense to explore and nurture your
own experiential definition of enlightenment. Allow the light
to shine.

Explore Enlightenment

Is creating my own definition of enlightenment merely relativism? Every definition of enlightenment is subjective and relative. The opportunity to explore your personal experience of enlightenment is a unique feature of the Universe. We tend to expect objectivity and external standards in religion and then get locked into those beliefs. Consequently, we lose sight of our own authority on such precious issues as enlightenment and happiness. Reclaim your authority to be happy and be enlightened.

Spiritual Sovereignty

To live in full spiritual sovereignty requires deep introspection and very keen insight into self. Spiritual sovereignty does not mean simply to do whatever you want. You need to know what you are, what you want, what you wish to feel and how you choose to express life. This is not mere egoism; indeed, it's not egotistical at all. This is piercing insight into the nature of the Universe as it manifests in that person you usually refer to as yourself.

Enlightenment is what we Are

Enlightenment does not depend on following this scripture
or that doctrine, this god or that guru. You are
enlightenment. You are happiness. These are states of
Essence. To the degree that we forget these truths, is the
degree that we suffer states other than happiness and
enlightenment.

Inner Truth is Sovereignty

Life is all about remaining true to your inner core, your inner
truth, your internal knowing that you choose to be happy.
Life requires no rewards, acknowledgements or anointments
from any higher being. Inner truth is Sovereignty.

The Inner Core that Radiates

It is your choice to accept or reject, criticize or embrace, this
description of happiness and enlightenment. Whether you
acknowledge or refute this understanding of enlightenment,
that is your decision. Such judgments have nothing to do
with the inner core that radiates so abundantly within.

Step Away

By assuming any identity, I take a step away from
Universality.

The Ego Feeds

Every opinion reinforces the ego. Every criticism reinforces the ego. Whether giving or receiving, the ego feeds.

The Eschewal of Concepts

I still feel compelled to explain my concept to friends, when indeed it is the eschewal of concepts that I seek to live. Having a concept and identity are foundations for the limited self to perch. In the absence of goals and concepts resides the infinite Essence of the Universe pulsating and radiating.

The Curriculum of Life

You are the curriculum of this life. Even if 'you' do not exist.

Wind, Rain and Gravity

Observe how breathing occurs by itself; there is breathing, but no conscious breather. Similarly, discern how thinking occurs by itself; but there is no thinker. Now, purposely think of a cat… of swimming… of coffee… and note how the thinker is temporarily in control. Then return to unmitigated observation of the natural rise of thoughts as they occur unbeckoned, as natural as wind, rain and gravity.

The Black Market

Seeking credit is akin to getting a loan on the black market. It makes us more vulnerable to the lender of credit who can extort any interest demanded. Do not seek one gram of credit for anything you do. Rather, give yourself credit for all that you do… self-financing.

Junk Food

Seeking attention is analogous to eating junk food. Any attention or junk received is of negative nutritional value. It even makes us hungrier. Seeking attention or acknowledgement leaves us vulnerable to even greater disregard or disrespect because power always remains in the hands of the other. Seek not one more gram of attention. Pay attention and acknowledge your own efforts: self-nurturing.

Mere Wisdom

Mere wisdom is where there is no wise one. Mere
observation is when there is no observer. This is where there
is no mind, no matter, no Universe.

Competition between Right and Wrong

I recognize how I must always be right, and therefore, you
and everybody else must be wrong. There's so much
competition in my head! No wonder I am so defensive. I
take a deep breath and relax the tension. This is not the
prettiest of insights, but it touches on real thoughts as they
arise.

The Yoga of Balance

Learn and practice the life postures that are opposite to your
given nature. If it is your nature to work, balance it with play.
If it is your nature to be lazy, learn to develop momentum. If
you are already pushy, learn to pull back and relax. This is
the Yoga of balance.

Balance with Nature

Create a balance between what nature has given you and what you return to nature. Are you usurping life from any other being?

Intuitive Yoga

'Think' Yoga before beginning a session. How does it feel to think Yoga? Prime the mind with the tasks, mental efforts and spiritual aspirations of the practice. Think it through and activate it mentally and spiritually. Although each session may be called a routine, it must never be allowed to become routine. Rather, Yoga should flow intuitively.

Nobody doing Yoga

'Think' a posture before entering it. Enter the posture and be present in it. 'Be' the posture. Be sure the mind is not wandering. The mind and body must both enter the posture until there is 'nobody' doing Yoga. Yoga uses the body posture to nurture a mental-spiritual state that transcends the importance of the body.

Yoga Grace

Following the inner flow of energy for our practice adds Grace to Yoga more than merely striving to perform some posture. Life itself is a long term Yoga asana.

Pushing Reveals the Ego

Pushing towards perfection in Yoga reveals the ego. This approach sacrifices elegance and flow, destroying the Essence of the practice. The pushing disappears when the pusher is gone. Prana minimizes the pusher in tune with the movement of the Universe.

What is the Essence of Yoga?

Joy is the supreme measure of mastery. I have stopped concerning myself with time, duration, repetition or perfection in Yoga. Although these may provide a goal or guidance, they also distract from the Essence of Yoga. Universal Consciousness is much more concerned with the joy of Yoga than with achieving physical goals. The Universe measures Yoga only in smiles. A spontaneous inner smile confirms achievement more than reaching goals or recognition of success.

Universal Yoga

Maintain the perspective from the Universe in every Yoga posture. Nurture the presence of the Universe as you allow the personal presence to surrender.

Spiritual Maturity

Develop spiritual maturity by taking responsibility and assuming authority for the whole process of mental-physical-spiritual development.

Commitment

Should we have goals when practicing Yoga? The point of Yoga is not to achieve the goal. The point is to maintain a regular, healthy commitment and enjoyment of the process of Yoga.

Ego Yoga

'Ego Yoga' has become very popular in recent decades. Ego Yoga is the latest trend in world Yoga practice. Doing a head stand with the left toe in the right ear and the right toe in the left ear is scarcely the goal of Yoga. Taking muscular and elegant photos of yourself in some challenging asana demonstrates the ego much more than it reveals Grace. The Essence of Yoga defies all photography, for the Essence of Yoga scarcely even concerns the body.

Internal Joy

Maintaining joy in Yoga is the only real goal. Joy is not something that any teacher or Guru can assign, describe or define. Joy cannot be photographed. Joy remains your internal, personal sagacity.

Respect the Edges of your Potential

Feel the whole body during and between Yoga postures. Slow down, without pushing, and gently do what you can each day. Develop deep breathing by slowing down the whole process. Respect the edges of your potential as it evolves through practice.

Posture for Life

Yoga is not merely a physical pose; Yoga is a posture for a holistic life.

All you Are

You are breathed (by Prana)
You are lived (by the life force)
You are moved (by Yoga)
You are conceptualized (by Universal Consciousness)
You see, that's all you are

'Who' is doing Yoga?

The Universe is nurturing itself through postures of the body
and with deeply nourishing therapeutic breathing. Asana,
without nourishing breath, is merely a 'posing,' a superficial
sculpting of the body, ignorant of the profound Essence of
the healing Yoga.

Healing Yoga

Deep breathing brings purified oxygen. Deep breathing with
therapeutic and nourishing intention stimulates healing. This
increases positive energy and enhanced flow. This is how the
Universe revives and heals itself via the body-mind of a
human. Bring the scattered pieces of the Universe back
together and heal the fragmentation.

Yoga Practices You

Allow the Yoga to practice you, just as Universal
Consciousness conceives you into existence.

In Tune with Infinity

Universal Consciousness is not limited to the 'you.'
Consciousness is infinite. Only a fragment of the ubiquity of
Consciousness is observed through individual eyes. Allow
yourself to see the whole Universe by shedding your ego-
focus. This will bring you into tune with infinity.

Posture of Authority

The intention of releasing the ego during a Yoga posture is
the Essence that gives the posture its authority.
Commitment to a posture empowers it, while weakening the
ego. This transforms our energy by raising our intentions to
a higher centre in our being. Be careful though, for
excellence in asana may promote the ego's sense of
accomplishment. Remember, it's not you that is doing Yoga.
Rather, Yoga is doing you.

Innervation of the World

For years, asanas have taken me by the hands and feet and
led me up and down the spine... Yoga innervates the world
to flow through these muscles and tendons with never a
thought as to 'who' is in the pose.

Reunion

Let's see where the path of self and non-self joyfully reunite.

The Orchard

As the tall wild flowers of the orchard spread their seeds at autumn's end, so has the Universe employed this human voice to share its words across the seasons.

Already Light

He is no longer searching for the greatest teachings that would lead to his enlightenment, for there is no searching when there is no path. The greatest technique is the absence of technique; effortless, with no 'one' to conduct the search in the Universe that is already light.

Yoga that is not Yoga

Surrender into the pose… until you cease to identify with
that body… until you cease to identify with that mind…
until you cease to identify with that pose… until you cease to
identify with that surrender: that is the Yoga that is not
Yoga.

Manifestation

What is the nature of Universal Consciousness?

It is THE mind that speaks / thinks / feels through
manifestation in all beings. You are neither something nor
nothing. You express Universal Consciousness in a certain
way that your friends recognize as you. You simply express
and that's cool. Now, when you take credit as the author,
there, you are mistaken. All credit for all deeds throughout
history is the expression of the varied patterns of Universal
Consciousness.

Colours Simply Are

'You' are one expression of Universal Consciousness. You
are neither right nor wrong. Similarly, all other voices are
neither right nor wrong. Indeed, the voices are usually
conflicting and contradicting each other. Why? The Universe
is profusely multi-faceted. That is its nature. The colours of
the Universe are neither right nor wrong. They simply are.

Credit Boosts the Ego

You are a personification of Universal Consciousness with
your colour and flavour for which, most often, you gladly
accept credit. And you seek more credit, don't you! And that
credit boosts the ego, which will eventually bankrupt you
spiritually.

The Voice

The voice of Universal Consciousness can be spoken
through the Universe, matter, mind or god, angels or spirits,
who allow the voice to speak through them. All of those
voices are actually the same; they simply represent different
dialects or constructs, paradigms or interpretations.

The Gift of Consciousness

Consciousness is a gift. You are Consciousness. You and
your friends are expressions of Universal Consciousness as
you create the Universe through poetry of every language
and paint of every colour. Reciprocally, paint and poetry
create you. You create the Universe, while also perceiving it
and being it.

The Universe is Mind

Is it appropriate to enter Universal Consciousness? Once
you realize that Universal Consciousness is all that you are,
you will experience this perspective as totally natural.

Explore the Chakras

What are the benefits of meditation on the chakras? Chakras are levels of mind corresponding to stages of human development and Universal evolution. Meditation on the chakras is a helpful technique to understand, conceptualize and navigate the dimensions of your being and the totality of the Universe. Chakra meditation helps you understand the complexity of Universal Consciousness as manifest in humans. Chakras are the key to exploring the mind-body-Universe phenomenon.

Infinite Colours

Universal Consciousness always is already everywhere, in as much as it has any physical location, which is only relative. When Universal Consciousness expresses itself, life arises. Life is the expression of Universal Consciousness through matter. Each life expresses one of the infinite colours and textures of Universal Consciousness.

What Distinguishes Life from Death?

Life is matter animated by Universal Consciousness. When Universal Consciousness leaves, life departs. In life, the elements of matter are ignited by Consciousness. Near death, Consciousness withdraws and the entropy of matter sets in. At death, matter and Consciousness part ways; each returning to the whole.

What is Death?

Death is matter devoid of Universal Consciousness. Death means returning to the Universal source: earth, fire, water, air and Consciousness. It's not that you die and then Consciousness leaves; rather, Consciousness fades and death ensues. Consciousness returns to the original Universal field. Your mother was one expression of the voice, colour and sound of the Universe. She expressed its love, hopes and worries. She shared that with the world while Consciousness was shining through her. You personalize this as 'mom' just as we personify all beings. We are all personifications of Universal Consciousness.

¡Vivo la vida!

What is the most important thing in my life?

Live your life. Just don't take credit for it. Remember, "¡Vivo la vida!" as Señor Ameriko exclaimed years ago in Perú. His was the voice of the Universe speaking. I need to hear this again to allow the voice of the Universe to resonate within me and be expressed through my personal vision.

Patterns of Behaviour

What is the nature / Essence / reality of the physical Universe?

Let's consider the large-scale 'pattern of behaviour' of the Universe. The Universe is not exactly a 'shape' as you might think. Physical matter self-organizes into patterns of relative solidity that are based on belief, concepts or expectations. This parallels the way that ego is a pattern of behaviour that becomes solidified through the concept of self. These patterns are perceived by participants who perpetuate the seeming solidity by virtue of their responses, reactions, attitudes or perspectives of the world.

Reciprocal Causation

The causation of perpetuation is not one-way. Rather, there is continuous reciprocal causation between 'solid matter' and mind (Universal Consciousness). Actually, mind 'perceives' matter as much as it 'creates' matter. Matter and mind are continuously causing each other to behave, respond, control, and measure each other in recognizable patterns of behaviour. So, yes, a flat earth is a potential behaviour in the Universe, just as much as a round earth. The relative 'shape' depends very much on those who create it through mind.

Do you want a Solid Reality?

Sorry, reality is not solid in that way. Reality is as much what you project / expect as it is what you perceive / conceive. When earthly Consciousness (of the masses of people) reaches a critical mass – it can 'shape' society, or 'shape' the earth to match expectations and accord with various measurements of it. By itself, in 'strictly physical terms,' the Universe has no beginning or ending and the earth is neither round nor flat because they don't faithfully exist in strictly physical terms. The earth exists as a dynamic between the masses of minds that perceive / conceive it and the behaviour of matter in response to the creation / perception and projection / conception of its observers / creators / destroyers.

Dynamics

The dynamic interplay between mind and matter accounts
for continual change as you perceive it and create it. The
permutations of matter reciprocally cause changes in
personal and mass Consciousness. For example, the subjects
you probably consider to be fact-based empirical realities
such as history or geology are actually responding /
reciprocating between matter and mass Consciousness.
Humans do not merely write or re-write history; they actually
create or re-create it. Reciprocally, history creates us.

Grace of Light

Are you ready to receive the Grace of enlightenment?
Enlightenment means the Universe is allowed to shine
through you if 'you' allow it to shine. Be present and
receptive with your whole body-mind and the Universe will
be heard. Enlightenment is always here, but for the noise of
'you' it is not always heard.

The Universe Shines

It's not that people become enlightened. Rather, the
Universe shines through people.

The Will of the Universe

The will to become enlightened is the will of the Universe.
People may experience it as a vague intuition. As you learn
to trust intuition, more and more light can shine through.

Spectrum of Light

So, am I enlightened?

You have always been enlightened, but you have not noticed.
You've been busy seeking credit rather than noticing the
light. Enlightenment is not a black and white issue. Rather,
it's a spectrum of permeability that inversely varies with the
size of the credit-seeking ego.

Surrender to 'Failure'

The way to arrive at the hour of light is by renunciation of
maniacal efforts to understand. Surrender to 'failure.'
Acceptance of failure triggers a relaxation in the defences of
the ego. Call it humility. This allows the light to shine
through. Remember, be wholly present, feeling the whole
body vis-a-vis the whole body, and be aware of mind via the
mind. Don't push; just be; allow the wisdom to be heard.

Here

What is this Ego?

The ego is a pattern of Universal Consciousness which is
stuck in a rut of expressing itself in a particular manner,
forgetting that it is actually capable of expressing any pattern
of possibility in the Universe.

'Who' becomes Enlightened?

If there is no true 'self' then 'who' becomes enlightened?

Nobody becomes enlightened. Rather, more light is allowed
to shine through the eyes of the creatures, observers and
participants in life.

'Who' must be Reborn?

'Who' must be born again and again if we have failed to
become enlightened?

'You' are not reborn; rather, the pattern that manifests in the
present mind-body phenomenon will re-assert itself in some
new body-mind. The pattern repeats, hopefully with a little
more light each time. But still, there is no 'you' to be reborn.

Creating a Kinder World

Should we advocate for the rights of animals? Yes, this saves
lives and decreases acts of violence. Protecting animals
allows more light to shine through the eyes of the beings of
earth. Consciousness shines through the eyes of all beings.
To kill animals or to hire other people to kill them destroys
that channel of light. Animals manifest myriad expressions
of Universal Consciousness. Kindness towards animals
creates a kinder world.

The Voice of Life

Advocating animals' rights is to express the love of life that
is striving to become the benchmark of society. Yes,
advocate compassion and rights for animals, but take no
credit. Just allow the voice of life to speak through you.

The Eyes and Ears of the Universe

The Universe observes, reviews and monitors its evolution
through the eyes, ears and senses of its sentient beings. To
harm or kill any of those beings is a form of self-destruction
that hampers the evolution of Universal life force.
Consciousness is striving to evolve, to mature and to
overcome violence.

What is the Consciousness of Plants?

Plants are an expression of Universal Consciousness. They project life and light, colour and flavour into the physical Universe to nourish the bodies, nurture the souls and purify the hearts of its mobile creatures.

Transforming the Light

Plants are alive; so, is it alright to eat them? Be aware that the life energy of plants is transformed through you as the light and life of the Universe. Conversely, eating corpse-foods is a futile effort to recycle death and darkness into life and light. Eat red, orange, yellow, green, blue, indigo and violet. This allows the rainbow of life to shine through you.

Eating Death

Eating corpses is ingesting death and darkness. This does not nurture life and light. Consuming death handicaps your ability to allow the full spectrum of the light and love of the Universe to shine through you. Dead animals in your body darken the temple and dull the light of Consciousness that can blossom within you.

Eat Sunshine

Plants are the transformed light of the sun: eat that sunshine!
Indeed, plants shine the light of Consciousness because they
are more purely transparent than people. Plants are sunshine
Consciousness. Eat sunshine fried rice.

Addiction

Why don't some people respect the lives of animals?

They are unable to allow the light of life to shine through
them unless it has been sanctioned by religion or culture.
Many people remain indifferent to the obvious murder of
animals for their meals. They may be blinded by dogma or
trapped in a pattern of belief and behaviour due to inner
darkness. The body-mind denies the light that wishes to
shine through them. Darkness, blindness, rationalization and
indifference are symptoms of the addiction of eating flesh.

Graced by the Perseverance of Light

Do the wise ones arrive at enlightenment through their efforts on the path, or through Grace? How could we truly know, other than faith?

Wise ones create a path as much as discover a path. Each path is one expression of the Universe to make itself understood. Each path may be internally consistent, yet it is not a fixed objective realty. The wise ones demonstrate abundant Universal Consciousness shining through them. They are Graced by the perseverance of the light to make itself known.

Subsequently, the teachings of the wise ones take the form of human language and constructs. The paths of the wise ones are not believable simply because they are real; rather, belief makes them real. This is where the real trouble begins. Transmission of the path becomes reified and people consider it to be absolute, exclusive reality. Sadly, the path becomes fundamentally ossified and stagnant.

To Hear the Voice of Life

Religion is neither right nor wrong. Each religion is a
historical and cultural expression of Universal
Consciousness. Each is a system by which to hear the voice
of life and perceive the light of the Universe. A religion is
considered the 'truth' because people believe in it, more so
than people believe in it because it's the truth. Belief makes it
real.

Spiritual Dynamics

Religion 'works' and that validates it for many people. At the
same time, religion can trap belief / perception / creation in
a fixed pattern that becomes solidified and inert. Ultimately,
living religion needs to evolve into a dynamic pattern of
perception, projection, creation and manifestation in order
to thrive and benefit all of life on Earth. All life; not just
yours.

The Impermanent Truth

Even the 'ultimate truth' is impermanent because truth itself
is a finite human concept. Truth is permeable, changeable,
temporary and conceptual. Systems of truth are human
constructs that attempt to articulate what is beyond human
expression.

The Notion of Truth

The very notion of truth is a human convention. It is a human construct that aims to make sense of an enigmatic world. Truth is relative to the context of culture, perception and Consciousness of the masses at a given time and place in history. If there were such a thing as an absolute Universal truth, it wouldn't be in words, or concepts, or even humanly explicable. Truth is…

The pink flower
Of the ginger plant blossoming
Beneath the tamarind tree

Truth Incarnate

The incarnate flower is truth; it is not merely about the truth.
The flower is clear manifestation of truth because it totally
avoids words, concepts, cultures, history, philosophy,
religion, precepts and claims. The pink flower existentially is,
and when it dies…

The pink flower
Falls from the ginger plant
Beneath the tamarind tree

There's your truth. The flower, itself, the real organic flower,
is truth incarnate. Conversely, every poem, song or fable
about the flower is a human conception or interpretation.
The flower itself is the manifestation of the life force of the
Universe.

Nurture Silence

The mind usually wanders to the past or the future, and only
momentarily passes through the present. Consequently, the
power of the mind is weakened because it is haphazardly
dispersed. Allow the mind to become silent in order to
sharpen the focus of the Universe that radiates through you.
Then you will have the capacity to experience that the mind
is not even you.

Suspended Animation

Allow thoughts to arise in the mind and observe them.
Acknowledge thoughts without owning the thoughts.
Observe without becoming the observer. Monitor the
sensations of the body with the body, not with the mind.
Witness the body without being the body. Understand,
without identifying with the comprehension; allow pure
understanding without becoming the knower.

Quantum Influence

An observer influences the thing being observed as
demonstrated by quantum physics. Therefore, during
meditation, allow the Universe to make observations of the
mind. If you identify yourself as the observer, you influence
the outcome. You influence the thoughts, feelings and
matter of the Universe.

The Quality of your Soul

"Is there some inner secret of being Vegan?"

Let me share one secret: Once you become a Vegan, your entire life will flourish. Your heart becomes deeper than the society around you. Your mind becomes wider and more profound than you can presently imagine.

Becoming Vegan transforms your life at the cellular and spiritual level. This nourishes your soul to mature and experience wisdom through personal behaviour and experience of a purified body-mind-spirit.

This is the inner secret of being Vegan. It's much more than just the food you eat; Vegan nurtures the very quality of the soul.

You are the Universe

The Essence of meditative presence is to maintain
continuous recognition of the Universe as it manifests.
Sustain awareness that you are the incarnate evolving
Universe. Maintain that unfaltering perspective and deepen it
in meditation.

What is the Universe Thinking?

What is the Universe thinking right now?

The point of meditation is not merely to silence thoughts.
The point is to be aware of the thoughts (of the Universe) as
they manifest… without identifying those thoughts as your
own. They are merely thoughts… without a thinker. Remain
perpetually aware of the Universality of thought. Dwell
unattached to the individuality of thought.

The Ego has Free Reign

If your presence of mind is absent for a moment, the ego has free reign to claim the whole world as its own.

Universal Esteem

Through the healthy development of self-esteem, we eventually arise to the understanding that there really is no individual self; therein resides Universal esteem.

Before Dawn

Before dawn, realize, you are life, manifest. Before dawn, realize, all thoughts are already present in the Universe. As such, they do not come from anywhere. They are already there and you've just now noticed them. Silent practice with firm resolve allows you to perceive infinity that is already at hand.

Experience the Essence

Life may not necessarily have any meaning that can be understood by human intellect. Yet, you can experience its Essence.

Truth

Truth is an inside job.

Tools for Transportation

Don't stumble over the tools of Yoga, Reiki or meditation. Employ these tools with perspicacity. The purpose of these tools is to transport you beyond the need for tools… into the Essence.

To Nourish the Evolution of the Universe

The purpose of humanity, whether we know it or not, is to nourish the evolution of the Universe.

The Games of the Ego

Returning to one-ness is the key to transcending your ego habits and ego nature. Don't play any of your ego games, and don't play ego games with anybody else.

Nurture the One-ness

Come here to the silence frequently and you will remember the path back to one-ness. Nurture the one-ness in every opportunity from eating meals to pruning trees.

Be the Sentient Universe

Use every strategy that you can to be the sentient Universe and soon the ego will become dormant. Be Universal Consciousness and by default, the ego becomes silent. Radiate the Universal life force until it is your only way of being.

Twirling with the Stars

Late night twirling with the stars, dancing emotions, emanating kindness, exuding nature. Feel the whole body at once. Feel the energy field in and around the body. Converge with the whole earth, the whole galaxy, the whole Universe. Feel infinity; be infinite. Feel eternity; be eternal.

Insignificant and Supreme

Humans are insignificant; at the same time we are the supreme purpose of the Universe. We are life; not just the body and mind that we call self. Like all living creatures, humans are the life force manifest in a Universe of unknown, unfathomable origins and unknowable, unforeseeable destination.

Creatures of Awareness

All creatures of awareness represent the Essence of the
Universe. The Universe is aware of itself through the eyes,
ears and minds of its trillions of living creatures.

Genocidal Shame

What if bees were as complex in thought and emotion as the
human? What if chickens were as caring and wise as the
human? Would humans even know? What if every living
creature on the planet, from a fish to a duck to a cow was a
fully evolved being capable of thought, emotion and spirit?
What a shame it would be that humans did not know how to
communicate with these beings and could not learn from
them. It's a genocidal shame that humans allow and condone
the murder of trillions of earth beings. Only a small
percentage of people consider this murder to be immoral.

Self-Healing is Innate to all Beings

The self-healing capacity demonstrates the life force itself.
That which gives life is that which heals life. The capacity for
self-healing is innate to all living beings. Healing energy is
stimulated as needed because each living being innately
knows its own needs.

Genuine Health

Genuine health is best defined as wholeness. This implies a
proper balance of the essentials of health, which is
exponentially more important than the mere killing of
disease.

Innervation of Healing

Reiki works on mental and physical issues because it opens a world of hope and possibility for relief. Those who request a Reiki session initiate the healing process by demonstrating their openness to Reiki. There's nothing magic about it. It's perfectly natural. The hands of the healer do not 'transmit' energy as much as they 'innervate' the inner healing capacity of the individual. The capacity for helping and healing others is innate to all living beings.

Ego Denies Essence

The ego is not of an ontological nature. As such, it cannot be said to either exist or not exist. Ego is not a thing. It's not a noun. Rather, ego is a process, a series of events. Ego is an unseen belief, ideological in nature. Ego is a verb. Ego is a tacit denial of Universal Essence. This denial separates the holder of this belief from the wholeness of the Universe.

A Continuum of Elements

The Essence of the mind-body human is a continuum of
elements in varying quantities; namely, earth, water, fire, air,
sound, wisdom and Grace. The Essence of a tree is the
same; a continuum of elements combined in a particular
pattern to create what is known as a tree.

The Elements of a Symphony

A symphony is a combination of the same elements:

- Earth grows the trees that become the wood of
  violas and violins.
- Water flows as the sweat and blood of musicians.
- Fire is the melting of the brass that
  metamorphosizes into trumpets and tubas.
- Air blows through the brass and woodwinds.
- Sound resonates through all instruments.
- Wisdom is the genius that composes the score.
- Grace (the Essence of the Universe) is what makes a
  symphony sublimely beautiful, and inspires us to
  appreciate beauty. Gracias.

The Symphony and the Tree

The symphony and the tree never deny their Universal
Essence. Denying Universal Essence is the unique folly of
the human.

Staying in Tune

How can you stay in the present, in tune with Universal
Consciousness?

Learn to focus on the essential elements in the present
moment of your life:

- Examine earth through keen awareness of body
  sensations.
- Witness water in the tears of the eyes or sweat of the
  skin.
- Remember fire as it radiates throughout your body.
- Tune into air through consistent awareness of the
  breath.
- Follow the sounds of your own life force.
- Discern wisdom through the manifestation of
  thought.
- Celebrate Grace through the presence of God.

Meditation on Permeability

Remain aware of your elemental Essence. Recognize the earth element in your body as the world itself rather than as 'my earth element.' Understand water as communal water, and not as your personal, individual water element. Experience wisdom as Universal Essence rather than as personalized intelligence. Respect how permeable you are.

Dynamic Concentration

Create a stronger body and mind connection by focusing on physical-mental phenomena of the present moment. This creates a magnetic hold on the wavering mind. Maintain dynamic concentration.

Denial

After all of this, what separates you from the Essence of the Universe? Only the denial of Universality.

A Kitten or a Kite

Review again and again the elements of your body-mind
continuum. Compare these elements to anything else in the
world, be it a kitten or a kite; a cloud or a kiss; notice how all
of these are composed of the same Essence and the same
elements.

Wisdom of the Tree

The tree knows which soil will nourish it, how long to
produce leaves, when to blossom, when to offer its fruit to
the one it nurtures, and when to release its leaves to the
wind. Somebody may respond, "Bah, that's not wisdom!
That's just nature. There's no thought."

Wisdom is well beyond thought. The tree knows what to do
in the same way that an animal intuitively knows what to eat
or drink. Natural wisdom is not anchored in thought or
language. Wisdom is inherent in all of nature.

Being Present

Being very present helps you hear Universal wisdom. It helps
if you diminish the distractions of human thought by
quieting the mind to focus on the Essence.

The Nature of the Truth of Nature

If you wish to understand the nature of truth, focus your
attention on the truth of nature.

Universal Happiness

To be happy for no reason and without cause indicates one-
ness with the Universe. Pure glee, spontaneous singing,
dancing and sudden laughter reveal the flow of Universal
happiness in the mind-body that you call home.

Irrational Exercise

Seeking proof for or against the existence of God is a mechanical, scientific approach to the ineffable. To measure the ineffable is an irrational exercise. We may notice those who consider themselves to be most rational people engaging in this futility. What must be the case that proof and absolute truth exist in and of themselves?

This Universe Hinges on Belief

Could it be that the Essence of the Universe is belief rather than proof or truth? Proof and truth sound so strong, tangible and absolute, providing greater security to buttress our opinions. Meanwhile, belief sounds like a second-rate, intangible, subjective concept that cannot hold water.

This entire Universe hinges on belief. That makes it a totally subjective Universe in which God both exists and does not exist. This is a Universe that is not dictated by rational thought or logic. Why would a Universe be constrained by human concepts?

Illusions

If self is an illusion, then non-self is also an illusion.

Essence is Presence
in the Absence of Existence

Existence is based on the concept of an entity. Conversely, Essence does not require any concept of an entity. There is simply presence. Essence is presence in the absence of existence.

No Ending and No Beginning

When there is no ending and no beginning, you are in Eternity.

The Reciprocal Universe

Thoughts think us, more than we think thoughts. Now, consider the reciprocal nature of the Universe: We create the Universe through thought, which has been thinking us. We select the pattern of thought that flows through us and becomes our personality.

This parallels the nature of water, whose raw potential is liquid, solid or gas. Water has potential to freeze or flow, condense or stagnate. These states of water are neither good nor bad; they are simply raw potential.

Raw thought that arrives to the individual mind unheeded can be trained or 'domesticated' to follow a particular course just as the state of water can be transformed to fulfil a specific purpose.

We create a positive world employing happy thoughts, by choice. We create an angry world through selection of angry thoughts, which is also done by choice. The raw potential of thought is available for all types of worlds. We choose. And thus, we create the Universe.

The Primordial Paradigm

The self is the primordial paradigm through which
everything is filtered, selected, perceived and conceived. The
self considers these perceptions to be the absolute truth. The
body-mind-self complex is an ingenious filtering system that
selectively chooses particular details from the infinite raw
potential of the Universe, while denying, rejecting and
ignoring a range of other details. Through this process,
'reality' is constructed.

The firmer the belief or conception, the stronger the self
becomes. This makes the ego structure less permeable and
more rigid. This structural inflexibility further blocks and
filters out alternative concepts while reinforcing its own
structure. Eventually, the structure becomes ossified and
fossilized, reified and objectified, and the ability to change is
lost. Life becomes stagnant and all dynamics fade away.

Eternal Spring

You are
The eternal spring
Of the Universe

Here

Here

Now

Here

www.ingramcontent.com/pod-product-compliance
Lightning Source LLC
LaVergne TN
LVHW051520170726
843492LV00006B/1589